Mechanically Inclined

P9-CIT-976

Mechanically Inclined

Building Grammar, Usage, and Style into Writer's Workshop

Jeff Anderson

Foreword by Vicki Spandel

Stenhouse Publishers

Portland, Maine

Stenhouse Publishers
www.stenhouse.com

Copyright © 2005 by Jeff Anderson

All rights reserved. No part of this publication may be reproduced or trans-mitted in any form or by any means, electronic or mechanical, including photocopy, or any information storage and retrieval system, without permis-sion from the publisher.

Every effort has been made to contact copyright holders and students for permission to reproduce borrowed material. We regret any oversights that may have occurred and will be pleased to rectify them in subsequent reprints of the work.

Library of Congress Cataloging-in-Publication Data
Anderson, Jeff, 1966–
    Mechanically inclined : building grammar, usage, and style into writer's workshop / Jeff Anderson.
        p. cm.
        Includes bibliographical references and index.
        ISBN 1-57110-412-7 (alk. paper)
        1. English language—Grammar—Study and teaching (Secondary)
2. English language—Composition and exercises—Study and teaching
(Secondary) I. Title.
LB1631.A54 2005
428'.0071'2—dc22   205049918

Cover and interior design by Martha Drury
Cover image from Getty Images/Oliver Moest

Manufactured in the United States of America on acid-free paper
16 15 14 13 12 11   15 14 13 12 11 10

For Betsy Sue Anderson, my mama. The book you always wanted to write came through me.

Contents

vii

Foreword

You may not know it—yet—but the book you hold in your hands is a treasure. I say this speaking as a teacher and a writer. "How can this be?" you're asking. A book on grammar and usage? Will it hold my attention? Satisfy my curiosity? Entertain me? Enlighten me? Yes, yes, yes, and yes. Trust me, this is a book engaging enough to keep you awake on the airplane, enough to keep you turning pages into the night, and best of all—from a teacher's perspective—practical and informative enough to actually use, return to, mark up, quote, give as a gift. Put it on a handy shelf very close to where you do your lesson plans because you'll reach for it again and again.

Why? Well, for one thing, even though most of us feel relatively comfortable with grammar, usage, and mechanics (they are different, as Jeff explains so clearly), and very comfortable correcting others' copy, we do not necessarily feel at all comfortable teaching these things. This is easily understood if we think about it. While handbooks, even the best of them, are jam-packed with rules we must know to write in a literate and conventional way, it is rare for anyone to take the time to explain these rules simply and in depth, then provide examples (more than one, unlike those maddening algebra textbooks), and finally, offer us a chance to apply what we have learned—or think we have learned. Many people are willing and able to share conventional rules. The distance between people who will explain the thinking underlying those rules in a way that we understand and remember stretches out before us like a dry, vast wasteland of meaningless worksheets. Then, we come to the oasis . . .

Jeff Anderson is a true teacher, one who knows that to teach others well, you must teach yourself first. Reading Jeff's work is like having a conversation with a trusted coach. He makes it all simple for us. He makes it come alive. He offers examples ripped from the pages of today's most absorbing literature. And—here's the part I love most of all—he anticipates our questions and then answers them. This is hands down the clearest, most readable explanation of grammatical and mechanical rules and their applications that I have ever read. You often hear people say, "Oh, I wish I'd had that book when I began teaching." Absolutely. But even more, I wish I'd had this book when I began college. It was in college, after all, that we were finally expected to understand conventions inside and out. And that is just how Jeff explains things, inside and out. But sans tedium, sans lecture, sans drills. He's the sort of teacher about whom people say, "I wish my child could be in his class."

Here's the heart of it, for me, though. All of us who teach writing (and who write, for that matter) know by now the importance of teaching conventions "in context." We've read it in countless articles, heard it at countless seminars and conferences. We know the litany. It just never occurred to me— it came to me with a jolt, in fact—that I did not really understand what this meant. I do (and did) understand that conventions are not just about rules. They create meaning. They create voice. But in reading Jeff's book, I learned something invaluable: how to actually create that "context" we have all heard so much about, how to make editorial instruction meaningful, engaging, and understandable, even for students who struggle. Jeff Anderson patiently (and humorously) walks us through the steps of identifying problems, using students' own text as a tool from which to teach, providing examples through mentor text, and setting up practice that yields results. I have no doubt, none, that anyone following the methods and strategies so beautifully laid out in this book will see measurable differences in their students' editing—and drafting—skills.

What I love best about the book, what I philosophically embrace, is Jeff's clear position that conventions are not just about "fixing." They are about creating. We don't want to turn into obsessive editorial fiends, but neither can we afford to ignore conventions until the tail end of the writing process (when everyone is tired and eager to finish). Knowledge of conventional nuances makes the difference between "Let's eat Grandma" and "Let's eat, Grandma." Or, "I'm SO thirsty!!!" and "I'm . . . sooooo . . . thirsty . . ." Conventions are not just about avoiding errors. They guide us through text. They offer clues about meaning, challenge our imaginations, provoke images, conjure up characters in our heads, and affect what we think and feel as we read. Creative and skillful use of conventions allows students' voices to be heard. It gives them power. This—not a test score—is the real reason to provide solid and frequent instruction in conventions. Make no mistake, though. That power shows up everywhere: in e-mail, on a resume, on a job or college application letter or essay, in a poem to a friend or sweetheart, in a letter to the editor, in a first published work—and yes, in any on-demand writing situation. For after all, if you can write what people will read by choice, the world is yours. If you could give that power to your students, wouldn't you do it? You can. The secrets are all right here, right within the book you hold.

Leaf through this book and you'll discover all sorts of goodies we as teachers love: quotations galore (some real gems), delightful samples of student work, photos of students in action, checklists that are most definitely useful, and step-by-step directions on making your own instruction stronger, better, and more enjoyable for you and your student writers. Any of these things might entice you to buy this book, but you won't appreciate what a really fine decision that was until you sit down with the book in some quiet corner away from phones and computers and actually dig in. Then it will hit you, as it did me. I understand, you may say to yourself. I understand how to teach conventions in a way that puts my students in control of their own writing process.

This book is more than an overview of how to teach conventions, though. It's a modestly, beautifully presented example of how to teach, period. How to focus on the child, not the concept. As you read this book, you'll picture Jeff with his students. You will hear their voices. You will grasp what they are doing and why, and your understanding of writing workshop and the true, recursive nature of process will grow with every page. You'll feel more confident about the teaching of writing, and you will understand that conventions play a significant role in drafting and revision, not just in editing per se. A book that offers knowledge, understanding, and confidence all in one package truly is a book to treasure. Add humor to the mix and you have a book to cherish and keep. After all, anyone who tries to teach writing without laughing often and heartily is asking for trouble. As this is a foreword and not a chapter unto itself, I must wrap up. But here's one last thought. You really ought to buy two copies of this book because, sure as anything, a friend will want to borrow one, and you know how that goes.

Vicki Spandel
Author of *Creating Writers,*
Creating Young Writers, and
The 9 Rights of Every Writer

Acknowledgments

First, I thank Joyce Armstrong Carroll and Eddie Wilson for hooking me on a life-long study of writing through books, articles, staff development, and classroom practice. They gave me a way into teaching meaningful grammar with their "Four Ways to Use a Comma" in *Acts of Teaching,* which influenced me heavily in my search for a way into grammar that actually showed up in my students' writing. I went forth and permutated. Joyce and Eddie also taught me to acknowledge those whose shoulders I am standing on, so I will.

This book was inspired by the work of Harry Noden and his book *Image Grammar.* Harry's brilliant brushstrokes changed the teaching of grammar forever for me and countless others. He has been generous and supportive as I worked on this project, and I count him as a friend. He and Constance Weaver also sent me back to study the late Francis Christensen and his *Notes Toward a New Rhetoric.*

And it is Constance Weaver's seminal work *Teaching Grammar in Context,* which I read almost ten years ago, that largely informed my thinking about error and teaching grammar.

To William Strong, whose thought-provoking work and encouraging words helped me believe that I have something to offer to teachers—what a generous man.

Don Murray says we should leave a writing conference wanting to write more. Fortunately, this is always the case with my editor Brenda Power. Her nurturing, driving force ensured my success. Thanks to Bill Varner, who also contributed his grammarian eye to this project. The beautiful design of Martha Drury pulled it all together. Thanks to all the other people at Stenhouse, such as Jay Kilburn, Mary Ann Donahue, and Doug Kolmar.

Thanks to Barry Lane and Jeff Wilhelm for telling me what a gem Brenda is. Jeff's generous advice on how to write a first draft helped me finish the book.

Kylene Beers, thank you for publishing my first article in *Voices from the Middle,* which got the ball rolling for this book.

I need to thank many colleagues, such as Brad Whirt, Virginia Gordey, Dr. Paul Kelleher, Tanya Tilley, Debbie Grady, Moises Ortiz, Eric Tobias, Reverend Linda, Marilou Weir, and the late Susan Kemp, for their unwavering belief in me. Thanks to all the educators in San Antonio who have shared ideas and time with me, especially Dottie Hall, Tracy Winstead, Candace Anderson, Cynthia Tyroff, Carolyn Denny, Lou Medina, Aissa Zambrano, Kelly Sears, Beverly Prado, Miguel Ruiz, Andres Lopez, Greg Vesser, Joanne Angelini, Kathy Severyns, Cathy Byrd, Rebecca McCarly, Diana Rumfield, Mari Garcia, Patti Pelayo, Angela Sheridan, Suzy Lockama, and all the people who made me laugh and think and write and teach.

Thank you to my fellow New Jersey Writing Project trainers and my supportive colleagues at Rayburn Middle School. Thanks to all my students from Houston, Austin, and San Antonio whose voices permeate these pages. You make me stay in the classroom.

To my professors at the University of Texas at Austin, your brains, your zeal, your confidence in me ripple through this book and my career: Nancy Roser, Joan Shiring, and Elaine Fowler.

A special thanks to all my fellow staff developers at Write Traits—Ann Marland, Jeff Hicks, Shannon Murphy, Fred Wolff, Judy Puckett, Penny Clare, and Andrea Dabbs—and our inspiring leader, Vicki Spandel, for support and laughter, lots of laughter, and all the intellectual e-mails about reality TV.

To my Stenhouse siblings, Bruce Morgan and Aimee Buckner, thanks for the energy and the laughter. I look forward to getting our act together and taking it on the road.

To Nancy Considine for supporting my book habit.

And what about the writing partner? Thank you Gretchen Bernabei. I hope we keep writing books together. Your influence saturates these pages.

Mom, Dad, Jayson, Ellen, Edie, Dennis, Ben, and Sean, I am grateful for having you in my life. Thanks for the support and the love. You live in these pages, and you make me so very happy.

The Blueprint: Teaching Grammar and Mechanics in Context

Introduction

To those who care about punctuation, a sentence such as "Thank God its Friday" (without the apostrophe) rouses feelings not only of despair but of violence. The confusion of the possessive "its" (no apostrophe) with the contractive "it's" (with apostrophe) is the unequivocal signal of illiteracy and sets off a simple Pavlovian "kill" response in the average stickler.

Lynne Truss, *Eats, Shoots & Leaves*

It's fair to say we don't often hear an encouraging, tolerant tone toward grammar and mechanics errors in society or in many classrooms. "Grammar and mechanics are to be done correctly or not at all" is more often the underlying message. What about experimentation? Play? Approximation? Grammar and mechanics shape meaning, and as in all language endeavors, we must make mistakes to move toward correctness. Where's the bridge between getting started and stretching with grammar and mechanics and being wrong?

Let's get one thing straight. I am not a grammarian, nor am I punctilious about much. I've never been a language maven or even a stickler. My desk is piled high and every surface in my room is covered with papers and books. When I was a new teacher, I followed the three cardinal rules of effective writing instruction that I learned from Peter Elbow: write, write, write. Still do. As a new teacher committed to teaching reading and writing workshops, I knew that I wasn't supposed to use grammar books or worksheets, even though everyone seemed to. Still don't.

In my humble beginning years ago as a fourth-grade teacher, I thought providing my students with a workshop environment for writing instruction was enough for them to be successful. My classroom environment was carefully designed and my students' test scores were high. I helped teachers at neighboring schools develop literacy workshops, then presented my practices at district, regional, and national levels. But all the while I had a dirty little secret: I didn't know much about grammar and mechanics, and I wasn't exactly sure how to teach them.

Over the past fifteen years, I've come to know a few things about teaching grammar and mechanics to urban middle schoolers. One is the eighteen-inch rule. In Texas, we have a lot of Baptist preachers, and I once heard one say that the difference between heaven and hell is eighteen inches, pointing his finger to his head, then his heart. The heart of good grammar teaching is loving students' errors, loving their approximations. Lev Vygotsky (1986) taught us all about "pseudo-concepts," or budding theories based on initial impressions. Kids have a reason for doing what they do, even if it is flawed. I have found that, by understanding their pseudo-concepts in all realms, I can better teach them grammar and mechanics.

For example, last week I shared a picture of my dog with my sixth-grade student Vanessa. First, I need to tell you my home is my pride and joy—a 1920s Arts-and-Crafts-style home with hardwood floors and meticulous decoration. Imagine my shock when Vanessa asked, "Oh, so you live in a mobile home?" Not exactly a compliment in Texas. After stifling a chuckle, I asked her why she thought I lived in a mobile home. Vanessa pointed to the corner of my leather ottoman in the left side of the picture, "That leather seat is one of those benches on both sides of the dining room table. They have those in mobile homes." She used that one attribute and applied what she knew to come up with a theory about where I lived. Vanessa wasn't correct, but her assumption made sense.

In grammar and mechanics instruction, pseudo-concepts are overgeneralized rules like "Well, I am writing *its collar got stuck on the fence.* If I wrote *dog's collar,* I'd use an apostrophe. So I write, *it's collar.*" That pseudo-concept is based on knowledge about a language rule. A mistake like this from a student, and the thinking behind it, shows me where I need to go next in my instruction.

We will save ourselves a lot of frustration if we shift our notion of teaching punctuation and grammar to one of teaching principles instead of rules. Handbooks and English teachers often take a right-wrong stance. I'd rather my students take a thinking stance. Pseudo-concepts are stepping-stones along the way to concept development.

At the same time, I teach students it's important to clean up their errors. In the classic *Errors and Expectations,* Mina Shaughnessy says, errors "demand energy without giving any return in meaning" (1977, p. 12).

Though we know kids will get better at writing by writing every day, we can't ignore grammar and mechanics and expect kids will simply learn them through osmosis alone. High-stakes testing increasingly relies on knowledge of grammar and mechanics. We have to teach more intentionally. Grammar and mechanics are not rules to be mastered as much as tools to serve a writer in creating a text readers will understand.

If you've ever felt that you didn't know everything about grammar you thought you should, don't worry. Throughout the book, I weave in definitions as I use them, because I often became lost in texts that just assumed I immediately knew the difference between subordinating and coordinating conjunctions, appositives and adjective clauses, or the difference between a phrase and a clause—or how much my kids should or could know. Worse, some books used the old cop-out: Check any good handbook. Please! If you ever feel lost, check for a definition in the Glossary included at the back of the book (see pages 183–86).

First, I should define what I mean by grammar and mechanics. *Grammar* includes all the principles that guide the structure of sentences and paragraphs: syntax—the flow of language; usage—how we use words in different situations; and rules—predetermined boundaries and patterns that govern language in a particular society. *Mechanics,* on the other hand, are ways we punctuate whatever we are trying to say in our writing: punctuation, capitalization, paragraphing, formatting. Often when teachers discuss the six traits of effective writing, this aspect of language is referred to as conventions. In short, what are the things readers expect a courteous writer to do?

If you told me five years ago I'd write a book on merging grammar and mechanics with craft, I'd have laughed out loud. The man who didn't consistently use *its* correctly until he was twenty-six wasn't a prime candidate for a book on grammar and mechanics. Or was he?

In 1998, I moved from fourth to eighth grade. The new, high-stakes state writing test required students to know grammar and mechanics concepts that didn't emerge and self-correct in the workshop environment without some explicit instruction. In fact, in my inner-city middle school in San Antonio, Texas, my kids were stumbling as they tried to apply many basic conventions of writing. And now I had to teach complex sentences. How do you teach complex sentences? I wondered. I looked in the grammar textbook. It showed how to identify sentences as simple or complex, but that was about it. By this point, I was a voracious reader of professional journals and books, a habit developed during my master's degree work in literacy. None of these professional books about literacy workshop instruction actually said how to teach complex sentences—they just gave admonitions and advice to "teach grammar and mechanics in context."

What was a nongrammarian to do? Because I wasn't a writer who naturally and unconsciously picked up rules and patterns, my own struggles actually helped me devise methods for teachers who experienced conflicts about teaching grammar and mechanics. My weaknesses helped me understand how and why students developed pseudo-concepts about language, because I was occasionally confused by a few of those pseudo-concepts as well.

Don't worry. I have learned the rules by now. I am thirty-eight; otherwise, I wouldn't dare to write a book. Or would I? For as much as I knew about writer's workshop and the teaching of writing, I knew little about how to truly integrate the conventions of grammar and mechanics into my daily teaching. It's one thing to learn the rules, and another to figure out how to balance explicit instruction about rules with the daily demands of a writer's workshop.

When I taught fourth grade with twenty-two students, I conferred with students and shared what they needed to know on an individual basis. If a problem popped up all over the class, I taught a mini-lesson. Even then I merely presented concepts rather than teaching them. The instruction was scattershot, but the test scores were high enough that I thought it was enough.

But once I moved to the middle school, I had 150 students I only saw for fifty minutes a day. My advice was random and ineffective: "Make sure all your sentences aren't the same. Make long ones and short ones. Don't have run-ons." I'm sure my kids loved all the advice and admonitions! I was just like all the writing experts, calling out as I walked into my classroom, "Teach grammar and mechanics in context!" The grammar and mechanics I taught one-on-one or in random, whole-class lessons only went so far. I had to do more, and I had to do it systematically.

What's Important?

> We do not have time in our classes to teach everything about the rhetoric of a sentence. I believe in island hopping, concentrating on topics where we can produce results and leaving the rest . . . to die on the vine.
> Francis Christensen, *Notes Toward a New Rhetoric*

No matter how well-intentioned, if I deluge my students with too much of anything, they remember nothing—especially rules and the exceptions to those rules.

This truth gives me pause.

If we were to island hop as Christensen suggests, we should hop on the islands that matter, that give our students the power to write effectively. In terms of writing effectively, what really matters? What should we spend our time on? I can't spend the same amount of time on *who* versus *whom* as I do on *it's* versus *its*.

For example, in order for students to be able to play with or manipulate sentence parts, they have to be able to understand what makes up a sentence. They need to have a notion of subject and verb. Students need to understand patterns of punctuation and the patterns of sentences. But that's still a large territory, and it doesn't give a lot of guidance to teachers in trying to figure out how to best spend their time.

First, of course, we need to analyze students' writing, looking for patterns of error, but beyond that what matters most? Connors and Lunsford (1988) studied just that. Analyzing college essays from around the United States, they found twenty of the most common errors. Why look at a college study? Glance at the list provided in Figure 1.1. Familiar? Match it up with what's tested on editing and grammar examinations. Match it up with your state standards. With the exception of spelling, this list matches what my kids struggle with, but at the same time it narrows the wide black void of grammar and mechanics I felt responsible for teaching.

In developing my own list of common errors for this book, I took Connors and Lunsford's list, shuffled the items into like categories, then added a few other common errors I see my students make, such as double negatives, as well as important concepts I know my writers need to learn in order to express themselves. For example, I know my students make errors with punctuation and dialogue and need strategies to navigate beyond the simple sentence. Connors and Lunsford found that spelling errors occur three times more often than the most common error, so they threw spelling out of their tabulation. Spelling is a big area, and there are books by many experts that deal with the intricacies of spelling, so I didn't add spelling to my list.

The completed list, shown in Figure 1.2, contains errors and concepts clumped together in like groups rather than in order of frequency. Lessons that can be used to target the errors and concepts are listed in the right-hand column. All thirty-five lessons are contained in Part II of this book.

Because all students are different, choose lessons that will stretch them to their growing edge. Base your teaching on errors they make. Base your teaching on the strategies they need. No doubt, your writers will need many of the concepts in the list that follows.

My own thinking on teaching grammar in context has progressed over the years, from "If the students write enough, their grammar will fall into

---

20 Most Common Errors in Order of Frequency (Connors and Lunsford)

1. No comma after introductory element
2. Vague pronoun reference
3. No comma in compound sentence
4. Wrong word
5. No comma in nonrestrictive element
6. Wrong/missing inflected endings
7. Wrong or missing prepositions
8. Comma splice
9. Possessive apostrophe error
10. Tense shift
11. Unnecessary shift in person
12. Sentence fragments
13. Wrong tense or verb form
14. Subject-verb agreement
15. Lack of comma in a series
16. Pronoun agreement error
17. Unnecessary comma with restrictive element
18. Run-on or fused sentence
19. Dangling or misplaced modifier
20. *It's* versus *its* error

Figure 1.1 Most Common Writing Errors

The Sentence: A Way of Thinking

Concept/Error	Lesson
Fragments	Two-Word Sentence Smack Down Two-Word Sentence Search—Powerful Words, Powerful Verbs
Run-On Sentences	Dependent Vs. Independent—Adding On Without Running On
Dangling Modifiers	Only You Can Prevent Dangling Modifiers—Playing with Sentence Parts
Wrong or Missing Preposition	I've Got a Preposition for You
Double Negative	Register Swap—The Formal and Informal Registers
The Absolute	The Absolute Zoom Lens—A Think- and Look-Aloud

Pause and Effect: Crafting Sentences with Commas

Concept/Error	Lesson
No Comma in a Compound Sentence	Flipping for the Compound Sentence Pattern
Comma Splice	From Splice to Nice—FANBOYS to the Rescue
No Comma After an Introductory Element	If There Were an Olympic Contest for Sentence Imitating AAAWWUBBIS—The Subordinating Conjunction Bionic Mnemonic
No Comma in a Nonrestrictive Element	Basket Case—The Essential Nonessential Comma Rule An Appositive Imitation Is the Sincerest Form of Flattery . . . But Plagiarism Isn't
No Comma Setting Off Additions at the End of a Sentence	Life Detectives—Paying Attention to Detail and the Cumulative Sentence
Lack of Commas in a Series	Think Aloud—Commas, Are You Serial?

Pronouns: The Willing Stand-Ins

Concept/Error	Lesson
Vague Pronoun Reference	Marking Text—In Reference to Pronouns
Pronoun-Antecedent Agreement Error	Where Have All the Pronouns Gone? A *Kira Kira* Cloze
Pronoun Case Error	The Case of the Pesky Pronoun
Possessive Apostrophe Error	Apostrophe-thon

The Verb: Are We All in Agreement?

Concept/Error	Lesson
Subject-Verb Agreement	From Past to Present—It's About Time . . . and Effect
Dropped Inflectional Endings	The Verbs—They Are A–Changin'
Do and *Have* Agreement Errors	You Can't *Have* It All—If He/She/It *Has* Anything to Say About It Easy *Does* It—He/She/It Again
Unnecessary Shift in Tense	Who Took the Verbs Out? Verbs Still Making Students Tense?

Figure 1.2 From Common Errors to Teaching Targets

Adjectives and Adverbs: The Modifier Within	
Concept/Error	**Lesson**
Adjective Strings	The Human Sentence—Adjectives Out of Order
Adjective Clauses	Which One? An Adjective Clause Tells All
Adverb Clauses	We're in the Titles
Adverbs and Conjunctive Adverbs	Adverbs, Adverbs Everywhere—Strictly Speaking

The Power of Punctuation: The Period Is Mightier Than the Semicolon	
Concept/Error	**Lesson**
Misuse of Quotation Marks	Revealing Character—Tagging Dialogue with Action
Overuse of the Exclamation Point	Exclamation Degradation—Reflecting on a Point's Overuse
The Semicolon	The Semicolon—The Lone Separator
The Colon	The Colon—The Drum Roll of Punctuation
The Dash	Dashing—Simply Dashing!
The Hyphen	Hyphen Nation—Some Words Just Belong Together

Figure 1.2 *(continued)*

place," to a more directed, systematic approach. But, of course, as any desperate teacher in a test-crazed system would do, I have tried all the things that are not supposed to work, too. Just so I could know for sure, right? Not because I was tired, and it seemed to be less of a fight to just give them a workbook page or two. Oh, they were so quiet as they completed those worksheets and activities. I even got to sit down for a minute, but I always felt dirty afterward. Like I needed some sort of writing workshop shower to soak me in meaningful print.

When the Student Is Wrong, the Teacher Will Appear

I always remember how Nancie Atwell set me straight on spending hours and hours marking every error on every essay. She said marking every error did about as much good as yelling down a hole. The belief that if we correct them enough, tell them enough, workbook them enough, they'll get it, fails to produce independent editors.

Eddie Wilson shared with me, "If parents don't understand why you're not marking up papers, take a piece of children's art and stick a transparency over it. Then, start marking all over it, crossing things out, redrawing other parts, putting notes on it. Of course, everyone gasps. Then ask, why would we do this to student writing?"

Recent brain research shows that we learn in a weblike fashion—the web of context. The brain searches for patterns and simultaneously goes down many paths. I cannot teach in isolation and expect kids to apply it. I have to guide students by building an environment that supports writers in becoming their own critics, kids who look to punctuation and grammar to make their messages clear and interesting.

A New Paradigm: Grammar and Mechanics Through Writer's Craft

Instead of "drill and kill," instead of the mindless workbook pages, instead of the vapid test preparation materials, I use powerful literature and student writing to teach the rules of language.

One principle that undergirds my thinking about grammar and mechanics is that they are inherently linked to craft, and by making this link, we alter students' perceptions of what mechanics and grammar do. Instead of separating these into different craft and mechanics lessons, they should be merged whenever possible. It is this very idea of focusing on craft instead of correctness that so revolutionized my teaching of grammar and mechanics. In this way, we have kids crafting their writing with correct mechanics and grammar without even realizing they are learning them.

The ten minutes or so of writer's workshop I reserve for grammar and mechanics instruction needs to be filtered through these questions: How is this grammar and mechanics issue also a craft issue, and how can I use it to generate some authentic text? How can I look at it in the context of literature? And finally, how can I quickly turn kids back to their writing, so they can be on their way to becoming independent revisers, crafters, and editors?

I know from reading research that students can only attend to a certain number of things at one time. The more I make editing, correcting, and revising activities as regular as breathing in my workshop, the more independent my writers will become. The more I allow my students to be active problem solvers in these processes, the more they will be able to decide what, in fact, they should do.

What's my goal? Do we want students to identify and correct errors, or do we want them to know how to use the power of punctuation to create a message that is clear and beautiful? I want both, of course.

When teachers lament that their kids can't edit, revise, or correct their own work, I wonder whether there may be a missing piece to the puzzle. Do we ask students to edit before they have seen the patterns or know the concepts we ask them to edit for? We all want our students to have sovereignty over sentences, to self-govern their grammar, to have a license to edit, but what kind of training are they getting?

First and foremost, I teach the mechanics students need to know. Teach, not mention. Teach, not correct errors. Whenever my students aren't successful, I ask myself these questions:

- What have I done to teach this grammar or mechanics pattern?
- Have I immersed students in correct models? Visually and orally?
- Did I post an example (through a wall chart or insert pasted in their writer's notebooks)?
- Have I demonstrated how to use the mechanics pattern in a piece of my own writing?
- Have I modeled correcting this type of error in focused edits?
- Have I given students ample practice in editing this particular type of error?
- Is the item on the class's editor's checklist?
- Have I directed the students to edit their own writing for this type of error on multiple occasions?
- Is this mechanical error important enough to warrant doing all of the aforementioned work to teach it?

Once I give students a few processes, instead of loading them with a ton of strategies, they will be independent when they need to be. Without marinating in models from literature, without using mechanics to cook up their own messages, students will never be the editors or writers they could be.

What Is Context Anyway?

Teachers fear that if they have students look at one sentence as a whole class, they are breaking some writer's workshop law, that the craft cops are going to come beat them to the ground with a whole text. To put *context* in context, let's turn to *Webster's New World Dictionary of the American Language, Second College Edition*'s definition:

> *Context n. 1. The parts of a sentence, paragraph or discourse, etc., immediately surrounding a specified word or passage that determines its exact meaning.*

Other definitions say similar things about the surrounding words "throwing light on its meaning" or "helping explain its meaning." Context is about meaning. Any chunk of meaning is a context. The key is meaning, not length. We can zoom into the sentence level, or the paragraph level, and zoom back out to the essay level or beyond.

Instructionally, we make decisions about zooming in and out as needed. This view of context allows us to cut away the noise and focus on a concept, then quickly zoom out into a larger context once the pattern is seen.

All the workshop experts tell us to teach grammar and mechanics in context. Some teachers have become paranoid about teaching grammar in context—they believe that "context" means using whole texts only. They never cut away all the noise of an entire essay to focus in on one high-payoff grammar and mechanics concept or common error, never use the shortest possible text.

Our hearts are in the right place. In workshop we teach one thing a time, one thing kids can easily hold in their heads and apply. One thing we can scaffold. One shared experience. Here's where our heads come in. Use an essay to exemplify one grammatical concept? I don't think so. Truth is, there will be so many great grammar and mechanics things going on that it will be hard to focus, especially at first. So, workshop hearts and minds must meet in the context of a sentence. Taking the time to notice what effect the author's use of craft has on the reader, playing around with what-ifs, imitation, and permutation—you can do these things most effectively with a sentence or two.

Pulling It All Together Workshop-Style

To incorporate this focused approach to teaching grammar and mechanics into my writer's workshop, I didn't have to throw out what I was already doing. I just tweaked the processes of my successful workshop. I began doing the following:

- Using the shortest mentor text possible so that kids could cling to the craft and meaning without being overwhelmed by words and punctuation.
- Teaching one thing at a time and applying it to our daily writing encourages students to keep inventing and generating text while cueing them into specific concepts and strategies.
- Adding quick daily doses of grammar and mechanics experiences with short mentor texts and editing so that my students would have ongoing, shared experience with playing with and understanding grammar and mechanics.
- Providing rich experiences in the writer's notebook to apply and play with mentor sentences as new concepts were introduced.
- Giving students scaffolds in the forms of examples and visual inserts for their writer's notebooks to help them start and continue collecting, categorizing, and imitating mentor texts.
- Saturating my walls with visuals that provide reinforcement of the concepts introduced and used by writers. The placement and color of

these visuals reinforce key concepts that students need to know, helping them make connections and distinctions of meaning.

Why I Had to Write This Book

Over the last four years, I have been sharing my grammar and mechanics strategies and theories with other teachers. I've worked with teachers who only use grammar workbooks or test prep materials. I've worked with teachers who don't understand the underlying patterns and rules of more sophisticated prose. I've even worked with teachers who say in a slow Southern drawl, "I'm not mechanically inclined." I hope this book will help teachers who are unsure about grammar, as well as those teachers who are walking style guides.

It's no wonder we have a generation of teachers who don't feel confident about teaching grammar and mechanics. Maybe they were workbooked or diagrammed to death. Maybe their teachers avoided grammar and mechanics instruction altogether. Maybe they were led to believe that best practice in literacy instruction couldn't include explicit instruction in grammar and mechanics. Now, with standardized grammar tests from the fourth grade all the way to the new SAT, the bottom line has become clear: We have to find ways to teach students about grammar and mechanics at a time when they have less and less experience with the printed word.

The purpose of this book is to give teachers concrete ways to merge grammar and mechanics with craft in the context of meaningful writing. Kids can use these quick strategies in their own writing without ever cracking open a grammar book. However, students will still receive scaffolding on deciphering the code of our language.

Studying brain research, the learning theories of Lev Vygotsky, Harry Noden, Constance Weaver, William Strong, and all the writing teachers who fill my reference list, I searched to find what works in the teaching of grammar and mechanics. I taught and tweaked, tried and revised, until I had the base for lessons included in this book. Over the years, I have experimented in my inner-city classroom and discovered strategies for teaching grammar and mechanics in quick, well-selected doses.

I knew there had to be some research-based way to teach grammar and mechanics that would stick with my students and transfer into their writing—without resorting to what I had learned from experience wouldn't work.

Changing the prevailing negative attitude toward the teaching of grammar and mechanics is my mission. Grammar and mechanics no longer have to be the castor oil of writing workshop—something yucky you have to swallow before you can get to the business of writing. Grammar and mechanics are the business of shaping our writing, shaping our meaning, and creating effects that dazzle.

Sixteen years of study and experimentation in my inner-city classroom have led me to share my experiences as I continue to learn more about students and writing instruction. I hope what I offer can become a part of living and growing classrooms where options for writing (grammatical or mechanical) are shared, explored, crafted, questioned, revised, and enjoyed.

I intend for students and teachers to view grammar and mechanics as a creational facility rather than a correctional one. The teaching of conventions is about what punctuation can do to enhance the writer's message. Wouldn't it be cool if students thought of grammar and mechanics as play? If they had a "let's see what this does" attitude? This is the attitude I hope to cultivate with this book.

Moving from Correct-Alls to Mentor Texts

As writers, we learn most of what we know just by watching the pros, don't we?

John R. Trimble, *Writing with Style*

Often teachers fall back on grammar and mechanics textbook lessons and workbook pages for lack of something better to do. Many teach mechanics and grammar with daily correct-alls. Yet as far back as 1936, the National Council of Teachers of English (NCTE) found that the formal teaching of grammar and mechanics had little effect on students' writing and, in fact, had deleterious effects when it displaced writing time. Other teachers who know these methods don't work have fallen into haphazardly mentioning mechanics or, fearful of teaching grammar and mechanics out of context, teaching them only during the editing phase of the writing process. When this is the case, kids may only deal with grammar and mechanics a few times a year. Three hundred and sixty degrees from wrong is still wrong. I had to break open the "way it's always been done" and figure out why the tried-and-untrue methods don't work.

Canned Daily Correct-Alls

Are you picking up a tone here? It's true. I am not in favor of most daily correct-alls publishers create by the dozens. Correct-alls are the prepackaged editing programs that overwhelm students with sentences so riddled with errors that it is impossible to spend sufficient time on each type of error, much less see through the maze of corrections on the overhead. With correct-alls, only those already good at correct-alls get better.

Many correct-alls don't capitalize the first word of every sentence, nor do they have end punctuation. I have observed kids getting so numb with this kind of repetitive activity that they actually miss putting a question mark when it is finally needed. In a robotic, unengaged fashion, they make the same marks every day.

It's not rocket science. One sentence with ten errors to correct is problematic. How on earth can you discuss the errors? How will students pick up the patterns of correctness in language by marking up a sentence beyond recognition? How can teachers give the depth of discussion needed to address the purpose and effect of punctuation with so many errors? With what we know about the brain absorbing information visually, is it a sane educational strategy to have kids stare at something so wrong for the first ten minutes of class every day? Etching wrongness into my students' visual stores was not what I wanted.

To make matters worse, my kids did not transfer canned daily correct-alls into their writing. So why do them?

I found I needed to address more sophisticated errors. Middle school students don't need proofreading practice to capitalize the first word of a sentence or put a period at the end of a sentence. Their errors emerge when they struggle to shift gears from the informal communication of their world to the more formal or standard language expected in academic writing. Dialect issues, such as subject-verb agreement, double negatives, and dropped inflectional endings, are the gaps that may limit their access to future opportunities.

Mentor Texts: The Close-Up Lens of the Sentence

Are you weary of being a rule rattler, a constant corrector, an error eradicator? Do you poop out at parties? Relax. Let examples do your work. Telling kids about grammar and mechanics translates to students as *Peanuts*-teacher talk—the equivalent of blah, blah, blah. My lips are moving but nobody's listening. What do I do instead? I use a text as a mentor. A mentor text is any text that can teach a writer about any aspect of writer's craft, from sentence structure to quotation marks to "show don't tell." I let Gary Paulsen *show* my students about active verbs and short sentences. I let Patricia MacLachan *show* my students how to make phrases tumble off the ends of their sentences. I let newspapers, magazines, or any piece of literature make grammar and mechanics points for me.

Vicki Spandel (2005) gave a name to something I had been doing for the last few years: "sentence stalking." I am a self-professed sentence stalker. I am always on the lookout for great mentor texts: sentences, paragraphs, essays, articles, advertisements, and novels. I also constantly look for well-written student sentences, paragraphs, and essays. From posting a student's sentence on the door as a *Sentence of the Week* to using a piece of student writing as an example of correctness rather than error, sentence stalking goes a long way toward building goodwill in any classroom. Kids love seeing what other kids can do. It spreads the idea, "I can do that too." It encourages them to have their sentences taped to the door for everybody to stop and read.

When my student Christopher brings a sentence into class to show his friends, then I know he's got it: He can relish language and the way it is put together (see Figure 2.1). All students need to be sentence stalkers, finding them in literature and the world. If I can't find a student's sentence to make a particular point, I make one up. And, as quick as I can, I send kids back to creating and checking their own prose to match or imitate the mentor text examples with their own ideas.

Figure 2.1 Student Posts a Sentence

The Power of Short Text

I know kids need to hear the flow of language, its patterns, its cadences, its surprises, its syntax. Students who have limited experience with English need this even more. Whether they understand every word or not, whether they notice the way that dependent clauses tumble off the end of a writer's sentences, the flow of language is becoming imprinted and is more likely to come out of the writer who is consistently nourished and allowed to write his or her ideas on the page.

Reading provocative, very short text brings about surprising, thought-provoking student writing, especially when the readings are used as stimuli to writing. I read aloud, no matter how old the students are. The more behind students are, the more I need to read aloud from newspapers, novels, and poetry.

Jerome Harste, Carolyn Burke, and Virginia Woodward's linguistic data pool theory (1985) states that all of a student's visual and aural language experiences flow into that student's personal pool of data. Later, when communicating in oral or written form, the student will use things from his

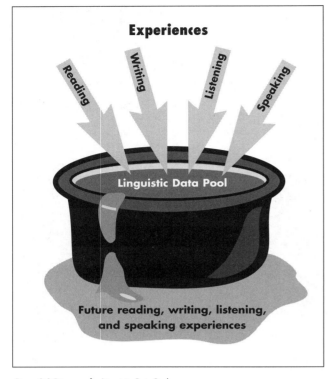

Experiences

Reading　Writing　Listening　Speaking

Linguistic Data Pool

Future reading, writing, listening, and speaking experiences

Figure 2.2 Diagram of a Linguistic Data Pool

or her pool in speech or writing (see Figure 2.2). In other words, every time a child hears a piece of literature, a conversation or a radio program, or sees print in written form, this data fills the child's linguistic data pool. That's an argument for a print-rich environment if I ever heard one.

Brian Cambourne (1987) used Harste, Burke, and Woodward's theory to explain why things children hear, from words to syntactic constructions, often appear in students' later writing or conversation. Cambourne calls the reappearance of these language experiences "linguistic spillover."

This theory also hearkens back to Mikhail Bakhtin, who argued that 50 percent of what we say is repeated text from previous linguistic encounters (Bernabei 2005). In short, what we hear and see will end up in our writing sooner or later. Therefore, the better the literature we read aloud to our students and the closer in proximity the reading is to the next writing experience, the more likely it is that a spillover of rhetorical techniques will occur in student writing.

After I share any short text, I ask students Barry Lane's million-dollar question (1992): "What sticks with you?" Its simplicity is its genius. Open-ended, this question allows students to explain what strikes them about a text, which, in general, are effective writing techniques. Processing what works in a piece makes it more likely that the stuff of powerful writing will spill over into students' writing. I am teaching my students to pay attention, to live consciously, to think, to analyze, to connect, to synthesize.

I have also found that typing the text of most picture books doesn't take that long. Then, as a class, we can look at individual sentences in even greater depth. We can use a text several times to look at several grammar and mechanics concepts in action and in context. Once the kids know what the text means, then their minds are free to attend to the other aspects of the text and to discuss the grammatical choices and their effects.

Zooming in at the Sentence Level

Ideally, grammar is a tool to help the reader and writer "see." Grammar focuses us in on the writer's point and "zooms in on" all the details that help enhance the point. As Harry Noden (1999) showed in *Image Grammar*, focusing on grammar's power to make movies in our readers' minds is far more interesting to students than focusing on a policy and procedures manual that ignores most of what is done in the literature students read. Noden (1999) and Christensen (1968) argue that success leaves clues. What clues does literature point us toward teaching? Useful grammatical structures cause writers to refocus, zoom in, notice, and grapple with information that will convey their meaning. Zooming in to the sentence level helps novice writers understand the connections between mechanics, craft, style, and meaning.

For example, when writers learn ways to add concrete details to a sentence, they begin to look at life more closely, more observantly. By teaching students how to add pictures to their sentences, we are requiring students to "see" their world again. Using details to create pictures with grammatical patterns sharpens students' observation and thinking skills.

Daily Doses: Using Mentor Sentences to Develop Concepts

To develop fluency in grammar and mechanics, students need quick daily instruction and practice. Ongoing shared experience with playing with and understanding grammar and mechanics is crucial. I take five or ten minutes—no more—to look at mentor sentences. I do it at the opening of class. I am not talking about a quick look at an entire book or even a whole paragraph. I found that looking at a whole text and merely skimming the surface of punctuation craft and moving on didn't help my kids internalize sentence patterns that fill professional, fluent writing. I had to be more intentional, more focused.

For instance, I take a sentence from a book we're reading or will read. Richard Peck's novel, *The Teacher's Funeral: A Comedy in Three Parts* (2004), starts off with a doozy:

If your teacher has to die, August isn't a bad time of year for it. (p. 3)

I simply ask, "What do you notice? What do you like about the sentence?" I highlight how the author crafted the comma to pause at just the right point, setting up the comedic end to the sentence. We connect the sentence's structure to one of the most used sentence patterns: a comma after a long introduction. There's more to notice—subordinating conjunctions, cause-effect— but the point is not to beat the sentence to death. The point is to get the kids to look at it, think about its effects, suppose the author's intent, and play around with the mechanics and see what changes.

"What happens if we take the comma out? Will someone reread it without the comma?" I ask. We debate whether we like the change or not. We try to imitate the sentence. At first kids will use too much of the original

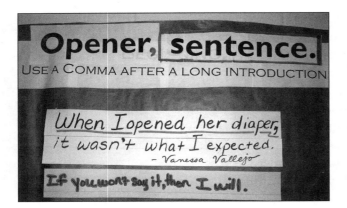

Figure 2.3 Openers Wall Chart

sentence when imitating. It's a necessary first step. One of mine immediately came up with this imitation of Peck's sentence: *If your teacher has to die, right now isn't such a bad time.* We place successful, original imitations on a wall chart (see Figure 2.3).

Another way to weave sentences into writer's workshop, when students have more experience, is to have students look back at two or three sentences previously studied and compare their structures. I know that when kids start looking at commas they become walking pseudo-concepts. They attach meaning to the wrong things. They develop hypotheses such as, "Any sentence with two commas has an interrupter in it." This can be true but is not always true. It's not the two commas that distinguish a sentence; it's the function of those commas.

Take this sentence from Eric Schlosser's *Fast Food Nation* (2002):

We cruise past block after block of humble little houses, whitewashed and stucco, built decades ago. (p. 10)

When I share this sentence with students, we discuss how the phrase *whitewashed and stucco* contains adjectives that add to the description of the *humble little houses*. We notice how moving the adjectives behind the noun meant that Schlosser was interrupting the sentence with details and necessitated that he set this interrupter off with commas. We note that we could take out *whitewashed and stucco* with its two commas and still have a sentence. Once kids start understanding a comma concept such as this, the first level of error is overgeneralization of the more sophisticated rule. They used to understand commas in a series. Now, when confronted with a sentence such as the following, also from *Fast Food Nation*, they say it's an interrupter just because it has two commas, even though they are serial commas:

Then somewhere a dog barks, the door of a nearby trailer opens, and light spills onto the gravel driveway. (p. 92)

As students conceptualize, they grasp onto markers to provide meaning. The commas in the middle of the sentence around a sentence part do make the part look like an interrupter on the surface, but we help students look beyond the surface markers of punctuation and more deeply into the meaning and the function the marks provide.

One way to quell this misunderstanding is to give students three examples to look at over time, introducing one per day over the course of three days. Later, we look back at all three sentences and cement the distinctions of function, meaning, and marks. The following three sentences from *Fast Food Nation* work well for this exercise:

> *We cruise past block after block of humble little houses, **whitewashed and stucco**, built decades ago.* (p. 92)

> *Then somewhere **a dog barks, the door of a nearby trailer opens, and light spills** onto the gravel driveway.* (p. 92)

> *All the trailers look the same, **slightly ragged around the edges, lined up in neat rows**.* (p. 92)

Figure 2.4 describes the three distinct patterns represented in these three sentences. *Note:* All the patterns are discussed at length in the lessons in Part II of this book. For my purposes here, patterns serve as conceptual categorization.

Vygotsky (1986) believed first levels of conceptual development evolve out of piles and heaps we try to form when grasping for meaning. Think of a kindergartener who sorts all the red buttons into one pile and all the black into another. At a higher level of sophistication, students need experience categorizing sentences, testing theories, and being wrong quite often, but we have to trust that students will move in the right directions when scaffolded and given things in small meaningful chunks.

Younger children may need to spend many weeks on one pattern, such as setting off an introductory element with a comma. One sentence at a time, students can begin to sort out which sentence patterns are like the others. Most important, they can distinguish between the functions of sentence patterns so that they can make them part of their individual sentence-crafting repertoire.

Sentence Patterns

Sentence	Category/Pattern
We cruise past block after block of humble little houses, **whitewashed and stucco,** built decades ago.	**Interrupter pattern.** This sentence shifts the adjectives, *whitewashed and stucco*, after the noun causing them to be set off with commas.
Then somewhere **a dog barks,** the **door** of a nearby trailer **opens,** and **light spills** onto the gravel driveway.	**Serial Pattern.** This sentence describes three actions that take place in a series. Since students often err on parallel form in lists of actions, highlight the similarities in form by underlining.
All the trailers look the same, **slightly ragged around the edges, lined up in neat rows.**	**Closer Pattern.** This sentence starts with an independent clause, which is followed by descriptions that tell about that sentence.

Figure 2.4 Sentence Patterns

Weaving Technical Terms into Instruction

What is the place of technical terms in grammar and mechanics instruction? There are no clear answers to this question. My best response is to share an example that shows the level of detail that is possible. Christensen (1968) argues that the sentence pattern "we can best spend our efforts trying to teach" is the cumulative sentence (p. 5). Before I define the cumulative sentence, let's look at some sentence patterns from literature.

In the cumulative sentence patterns below, notice how the bolded information that follows the base sentences sharpens the focus of each sentence.

> *Joel sat scrunched in a corner of the seat,* **elbow propped on the window frame, chin cupped in hand, trying hard to keep awake.** (p. 9)
> —Truman Capote, *Other Voices, Other Rooms*

> *John Laroche is a tall guy,* **skinny as a stick, pale-eyed, slouch-shouldered, and sharply handsome, in spite of the fact that he was missing all his front teeth.** (p. 3)
> —Susan Orlean, *The Orchid Thief*

> *Rising to his feet, he saw the field through drifting gauze but held on until everything settled into place,* **like a lens focusing, making the world sharp again, with edges.** (p. 1)
> —Robert Cormier, *The Chocolate War*

Basically, the cumulative sentence is a base sentence (also known as an independent clause), with a number of subordinate constructions, which are bolded in the examples above. What are subordinate constructions? Think of subordinate constructions as a string of modifiers, and modifiers are really just "describers." How would I put it in student language? The parts we add to the base sentence are what we focus our lens on, what we choose to focus on from the wide-angle shot of the base sentence (see Figure 2.5). *Lens focusing* is adding details, qualities or attributes, or comparisons to sharpen the image and deepen the reader's understanding of the base sentence (Christensen 1968). Lens focusing brings the writer's world into focus for the reader, making words sharp again with edges. Figure 2.6 gives examples of the three basic components of lens focusing.

The good news is that you don't need to share all these terms and options with your kids. It's not that our students need all these labels. However, it is helpful to consider the possibilities as a teacher. As I teach, I balance what students gain from learning the definitions or labels with what they may lose by delving too deeply into the technical terms instead of focusing on the craft of writing.

When you heard the term *cumulative sentence*, did your eyes glaze over? If you hadn't heard the term

Figure 2.5 Three Definitions of Cumulative Sentences

Cumulative Sentences

Independent Clause + a number of subordinate constructions

Sentence   + string of modifiers (describers)

Sentence   + lens focusing—zooming in on a
- detail
- quality or attribute
- comparison

Lens Focusing to Sharpen Sentences

Lens Focusing	Grammar Names	Literary Examples from *The Chocolate War* by Cormier
Parts or details	Prepositional, participial, or absolute phrase	. . . Brother Leon went on, **speaking softly** . . .
Qualities or attributes	Adjectives	He was aware of other players around him, **helmeted and grotesque** . . .
Comparisons	*Like* phrases	He needed a shave, **his stubble** *like* **slivers of ice.**

Figure 2.6 Lens Focusing to Sharpen Sentences

before, what helped you more? The definition? The examples? What if I'd given no examples, or only one example? Would you have seen the pattern?

Students learn by example. It's a cliché because it's true. We have to flood students with elegant examples, whether it be decking the walls with them or individually collecting our favorite words, phrases, and sentences. As teachers we have to focus our attention on literature and all of its possibilities.

Divulging Writer's Secrets Through Short Mentor Text

Students cannot become facile at writing in general and using conventions in particular if they do them only now and then—no more than I can get thin by dieting on Fridays.

Janet Angelillo, *A Fresh Approach to Teaching Punctuation*

Common sense tells us we have to do more than mention mechanics and grammar: we have to teach them. We can't expect our students to be flexible enough to apply these conventions if we don't cycle them in front of our students in various ways. By discussing the dash and figuring out what it does in authentic, well-crafted texts, students will begin to read like writers. Not just for style, but to see how writers achieve that style.

One good thing about daily correct-alls is that they do force students to consider mechanics and grammar on a daily basis. But the correct-all is rarely applied to students' own writing. It's all about searching for what is wrong with writing rather than what is right. Spandel (2003) frames the teaching of grammar and mechanics differently. In her book *Creating Young Writers*, she explains how she tells students that she has noticed they are ready for a writer's secret—a secret that all writers share that helps make their writing sizzle. The goal is not to point to what is wrong with their writing, but to encourage students by showing them what they are ready for now.

Leslie Hart (2002) suggests there are other reasons the brain needs repetition. He claims that input needs repetition, not in terms of drill and kill but a constant cycling: "Repetition within input can be valuable . . . because what a particular brain is not ready for at one time will be welcomed and utilized at another" (p. 145).

I know the value and necessity of recycling through all the mechanical issues. We have to cycle through them explicitly and intentionally several times for students to recognize the patterns. Until we build their schemata, students will have a hard time intentionally crafting their prose.

If our struggling readers need to see a word forty times to learn it (Beers 2002), then I'll make a leap and say students need to see grammar and mechanics rules highlighted in different contexts at least that many times to own them. If the kids don't know a particular structure or that they have options, some may not ever go into the realm of complex sentences or other effective rhetorical devices that separate functional writing from effective writing.

My experience teaching English language learners certainly bears this out. In fact, many of my students are flooded daily with oral models of language that don't correlate with what is considered Standard English. Students need scaffolding and modeling to hear the difference. It's not automatic for every child.

By the third day of school, the teacher who hates daily correct-alls wants to start a daily routine. Anyone who has worked with a challenging group of students—in other words, all of us—knows that routines create safe structures—brain research says it; Nancie Atwell (1998) and Lucy Calkins (2003) say it. Routines give our students something to count on, a place to hang knowledge, a place to share and explore every day.

Our kids write every day. I argue that they need a writer's secret every day, too. Students need to stare at and relish some well-written snippets of effective mentor texts. Every day we look at some writing to aspire to or imitate—texts that teach with their artistic punctuation or jaw-dropping grammar. An appositive becomes much more than merely a renaming of the noun it precedes or follows; it becomes a construction that allows a writer to combine sentences for rhythm and effect. One more pattern, one more choice to add to students' style repertoire. I let my students know I will share a writer's secret during the first few minutes of class almost every day. My students know these first few minutes are important; they know they must listen because they will hear secrets they will be able to use, taking the guesswork out of what makes writing effective.

Writer's secrets can be shared in several ways. I might:

- Lift a sentence from literature and let students tell me what is right about it, generalize some principles, and apply them to their writing

Figure 2.7 Students Copy Sentences on Sentence Strips for Posting

- Lift a sentence from literature and leave out one piece of the punctuation I've taught or make one usage error and have the students correct it
- Lift a sentence from student writing and imitate its mistake, whether it's a frequently seen error or a point I need to make
- Ask students to imitate a construction and talk about its uses
- Ask students to copy down an example of a rule from a mentor text, then discuss it, as in Figure 2.7

In my class, these five minutes each day will never include a sentence so riddled with errors that we could never deeply discuss the errors or the purpose for the mechanics. These quick warm-ups recycle or introduce information that the students need to know.

The key to the writer's secret being useful is that it is to be applied in writing that day, pointed to again during writer's workshop and at the close of writer's workshop. Evidence of the writer's secrets' use is processed again at the end. If it's not yet clear, then more focused practice may follow.

Remember that this practice is only a small part of teaching students about the uses of mechanics. It supplements and recycles deep instruction that is steeped in literature and application in student writing.

I find establishing a few minutes at the beginning of the class ensures that I hit high-payoff grammar and mechanics rules sufficiently. Kids' brains can only handle one new thing at a time, so I make sure this space doesn't become a catchall.

In addition, I provide order in my classroom—a structure and routine kids can count on. Katie Wood Ray (2002) says that we have to make our workshop routines and rituals as consistent as lunchtime. If I waver, the quality of my workshop suffers. If our kids are going to breathe conventions, inserting quick spurts more often and regularly is essential. We can't wait until the final copy to edit, but it pays off to take time for these quick spurts of well-selected craft and mechanics lessons that are based on student need and what researchers say kids need to know. In the next chapter, I'll show how this instruction is woven into the routines of writer's workshop.

Weaving Grammar and Mechanics into Writer's Workshop

The picture has a dollop of peanut butter on one edge, a smear of grape jelly on the other, and an X across the whole thing. I cut it out of a magazine for homework when I was six years old. "Look for words that begin with W," my teacher, Mrs. Evans, had said.

She was the one who marked the X, spoiling my picture. She pointed. "This is a picture of family, Hollis. A mother, M, a father, F, a brother, B, a sister, S. They're standing in front of their house, H. I don't see a W word here."

I opened my mouth to say: How about a W for wish, or a W for want, or W for "Wouldn't it be loverly," like the song the music teacher had taught us?

But Mrs. Evans was at the next table by that time, shushing me over her shoulder.

Patricia Reilly Giff, *Pictures of Hollis Woods*

As well-intentioned as editing marks may be, I know how most students see these corrections: as *X*'s over their souls, their desires, their thoughts. They view markings on their writing much like six-year-old Hollis Woods does in the novel excerpt above.

Often by the time students reach middle school, they hate writing. With the testing mania of late, the problem has only worsened.

Since grammar and mechanics are means to effective writing, I know the most important activity my students can engage in is composing text. Student

Figure 3.1 Student Writes in Writer's Notebook

writers should first experiment, imitate, interact, notice, and revise text without ever hearing these inspiration-killing words: *revision, grammar, editing.* Maybe we shouldn't even use the labels at first. Instead of telling students to revise, use correct grammar, or edit their mistakes, I begin by showing them how to create powerful writing.

For me, the writing process is not about students memorizing the names of the steps, especially since they are situation dependent. I try not to put my classes or students on what my mama used to call "auto-fold." After fifteen towels, you don't even pay attention any more, you just fold. The writing process begins with paying attention to experiences and recalling details, and ends with paying attention to our mechanics. I don't want my students to write on auto-fold.

Writing process labels, such as *prewriting, drafting, revising, editing,* and *publishing,* are dead without daily action, moving in and out of all the phases in true recursive fashion. It is in the experience, the interaction, and the trial and error that students learn how to write well.

I give students the advice of William Carlos Williams: "Write what's in front of your nose." I remind them, "You don't have to write about big trips to Disney World, though you certainly can. If all you ever write about are the things that happen to you at home or at school, that's enough. Ordinary things. You're welcome to write about anything, but the places and spaces where you spend time, that's where you'll know the details. That's how you can take readers anywhere, make them see and feel."

In Chuck Palahniuk's novel *Diary* (2003), the narrator keeps echoing these two lines, "Everything is self-portrait. Everything is a diary" (p. 3).

I often find that kids don't think their experiences are what I am looking for. When Ramiro writes about the time he hit his head on a brick flower box, it's important. Through conferring with Ramiro, I show my interest by asking questions, reveling in the specific details of how the blood in his mouth tasted like pennies.

I may even have him write that on a sentence strip and stick it up for others to see. "We've all tasted blood in our mouths, but the way Ramiro says it tasted like pennies, I can taste it all over again."

To help students see the connections between craft, revision, and mechanics, I start by nudging students to try new techniques, to reread writing, to hear and see beautiful and effective writing. Simply put, when students write, they begin to move toward correctness. And let's face it:

Writing is the life of the composition party. The best place to begin to make these connections is in the writer's notebook.

Writer's Notebook as Playground: Composing, Revising, and Experimenting with Mechanics

I think of the journal as a witness, a repository, and playground. It is where I begin things or bring thoughts to some kind of clarity.
Dorothy Allison, *The Writer's Notebook*

Writer's notebook, journal, notebook, living book, log, daybook, composition book—whatever you call it, writers of any age need a safe place to spill themselves onto the page. A place where writing won't get marked up by anyone except, perhaps, themselves. I let students have recess on the page, the sweet freedom to romp with thoughts, cavort with commas, and monkey around with syntax. What better playground do we have than the writer's notebook? This is the repository, the organizer, the placeholder, the idea catcher, the canvas to experiment and create on, the place to be wrong and to be wrong boldly. Writers' notebooks last.

Every thing in the writer's notebook is in process all the time. It is a place to return—to mine and refine, polish and relish, reread and rewrite. Maybe we should think of it as a rewriter's notebook, a reviser's notebook. Writing folders are great for holding finished pieces or parts of pieces in process, but the notebook holds a progressive record of the year and keeps all those scraps and loose-end responses sewn together, a deposit of gold that can be mined all year long. Students can return to its pages again and again, under your direction or of their own volition, to create and play with language by freewriting, going back and applying a new craft technique to a previously written piece, or quickly rereading a piece of writing for a targeted edit. But with all this playing, the challenge is to systematize what I teach when it comes to grammar and mechanics.

Setting Up a Writer's Notebook

Before students write their first word in the writer's notebook, it needs to be carefully set up for optimal use as a repository. I buy composition books in bulk at back-to-school sales and give them to students who can't find or afford them.

Over the last few years, I have formulated some guidelines that work for me in constructing the writer's playground. These notebooks are an essential tool to help my students become sentence stalkers (Spandel 2003).

First of all, I find it essential to spend a little time upfront emphasizing how important the writer's notebooks will be in our class. Students must get a sense of my reverence for the notebooks, my expectations for their care.

Once all the students have their notebooks, I instruct students step-by-step on setting up the writer's notebook:

1. Never tear out a page of your notebook. Never. I tell my students, "If you think you must tear out a sheet, see me."
2. Leave a fly page up front, just like in books.
3. Number pages only on the right-hand side, starting after the fly page.
4. Write the page number on the bottom right-hand side. This takes time, but it is a must. Think of the time saved later when a student can put a sticky note on the cover: *Read entry on pages 31–32.* Instead of dutifully thumbing through a notebook, I can turn immediately to the correct pages.
5. Only write on the right-hand pages of the notebook. Keep the left-hand pages blank for revising, rethinking, and tinkering with the facing numbered page. This saves space for the experimenting we will do with craft and mechanics in the notebook.

After students have numbered their pages, they are ready to set up sections in their notebooks. The following sections help students and me keep track of the varied purposes of a writer's notebook.

Beginning with Writing

The first section, "Writing," is by far the largest section of the notebook. Students freewrite, respond, prewrite, create, shape, take notes, glue materials from our quick daily writer's secret work, and play with their writing here. Each entry should be dated and given at least a one-word title with some sort of connection to the text that follows.

My students' most fluent and complex writing often comes in focused freewriting. In *Writing with Power,* Peter Elbow writes, "Frequent freewriting exercises help you learn to simply get on with it and not be held back by worries about whether these words are good words or right words" (1998b, p. 14).

Freewriting proper, in its purist Elbowian form, asks writers to write: "Simply force yourself to write without stopping for ten minutes" (p. 13). Focused freewriting, on the other hand, gives students a jumping off point. Perhaps this is a word or group of words, such as *neighbors* in one instance and *teasing* or *bullying* in another. The words may hold a theme, a feeling, a memory, an opinion, but they should definitely be connected to the text read as a stimulus. Writers are then encouraged to let their thinking guide them: "Just write. Go wherever the writing takes you."

If I tell my kids to freewrite, most students stall out after a few minutes, but if I read a stimulating piece of literature first, they write and write. Students often use techniques that the writer used in the stimulus text. I give them some ideas of what they can write about but let them go where their passions take them.

On the first day of school, I read an excerpt from *Autobiography of a Face* by Lucy Grealy (1994). Instead of lecturing on why we don't make fun of each other or bully in my class (or anywhere else), I share an excerpt from Grealy's memoir. Many reluctant writers don't want to share for fear of being made fun of. I find that establishing safety in the first day or so of class lays this fear to rest.

In the memoir, Grealy is diagnosed with bone cancer in her jaw. The cancer and chemotherapy eat away at her jawbone, collapsing her face. She's in great pain, her face is deformed, and now she has to start junior high school.

I ask students, "Where will be the hardest place for her to be?" I let them answer, giving me a lens into the places that feel least safe to them. Without fail, someone always says the lunchroom. I read aloud the following passage, stopping often for students to make connections to their experiences.

> *Having seen plenty of teen movies with their promise of intrigue and drama, I had been looking forward to going to the lunchroom. As it happened, I sat down next to a table full of boys.*
>
> *They pointed openly and laughed, calling out loudly enough for me to hear, "What on earth is that?" "That is the ugliest girl I have ever seen." I knew in my heart that their comments had nothing to do with me, that this was all about them appearing tough and cool to their friends. But these boys were older than the ones in grade school, and for the very first time I realized they were passing judgment on my suitability, or lack of it, as a girlfriend. . . . The same group took to seeking me out and purposely sitting near me day after day, even when I tried to camouflage myself by sitting in the middle of a group. They grew bolder, and I could hear them plotting to send someone to sit across from me. I'd look up from my food and there would be a boy slouching awkwardly in a red plastic chair, innocently asking me my name. Then he'd ask me how I got to be so ugly. At this the group would burst into laughter, and my listener would saunter back, victorious. (pp. 124–25)*

When I am finished reading the passage a second time, I ask the students, "What words or phrases stick with you?" I write their answers on the whiteboard.

"Why do you think the red plastic chair stuck with Anna?" I ask.

"Well, you could see a red plastic chair in your head when you read it," one student offers.

Freewriting Rules!

1. Write. Just write. Keep your hand moving. (The only way to do freewriting wrong is to not write or to quit early.)

2. Experiment with spelling, punctuation, and grammar. (This as opposed to "don't worry about spelling, punctuation, or grammar." Though we shouldn't worry about it, we should attempt to do the best we can.)

3. Go wherever your writing (thinking on the page) takes you. (If another story comes to mind, maybe that's what you should be writing about. Go for it.)

4. Be specific. (As you teach strategies like naming concrete nouns and snapshots, encourage those things in first-draft freewriting by praising them when read aloud.)

5. As Natalie Goldberg says, "You are free to write the worst junk in America" (1990, p. 4). (Students need to know that everyone has doubts about their writing. Allowing some writing to be garbage [Elbow 1998a] allows our writing to flow and good things to emerge.)

Figure 3.2 Freewriting Rules!

"So, adding specific details like a red plastic chair added pictures to Lucy Grealy's writing." Then we move on to larger questions and discussions that will serve in building a writer's community and writing with snapshots (Lane 1992) and details.

"Why do you think people make fun of each other? How do you think it affects others?" I share how I still remember mean things people said to me in elementary school—some thirty years later. "I will stand up against bullying in my classroom, and I expect you to refrain from it and stand up to it by saying cut it out or changing the subject. If it's a problem, see me, and we will work it out."

After sufficient discussion, I say, "Freewriting will be an important part of our writing in this class, and something you'll do often in your writer's notebook." I quickly explain how to freewrite, showing a transparency of freewriting rules (see Figure 3.2).

"Write *Bullying* at the top of your page. Skip a line and write about something you've done, experienced, or have seen happen. Start with the idea of bullying and go where the writing takes you." Pointing to the list on the wall, I say, "Remember what Lucy Grealy did to make pictures and images in our heads. Try to add specific details."

As we share, an important discussion ensues. One teacher I worked with did this activity later in the year, and told me the story of a girl, formerly the class punching bag, who started receiving anonymous notes in her locker. They were kind. The student told her teacher that people had almost completely stopped teasing her. We are building a writing community. But more than that, I am building a pattern that will repeat throughout the year. Read, reflect, write, share and process, re-enter and share, clean up. This is a mini-writing process that gets reluctant students writing and sharing.

Embedding Mechanics Instruction in Notebook Freewrites—*Bedhead*

I like to kick off my students' thinking about mechanics as special effects devices with Margie Palatini's *Bedhead* (2000). To show my students the power of punctuation for shaping meaning and voice, I read aloud *Bedhead*. In the story, Oliver wakes up with his hair going every which way, a seriously funny bad-hair day. His family tries to help him tame it, but alas, they are only able to stuff it under a cap. To make matters worse, when Oliver gets to school, it's picture day and he can't wear a cap.

I don't want to exclusively use one or two sentences to illustrate principles. It's important for students to see how punctuation works to hold and connect larger texts together. This charming picture book makes my middle schoolers laugh out loud. As I read, a few even repeat the echoed line, "like a cat's coughed-up fur ball." After the first reading, kids' faces light up and they initially respond with their own "hairror" stories.

While the topic is still hot, I write the word *Hair* on the board. I share about the time I shaved off half an eyebrow the night before I had to speak to four hundred teachers. "That's what I am going to write about. You can write about how long your sister takes to do her hair, like Ashley described, or whatever comes to your mind. Remember, with freewrites you start with the idea of hair and write the whole time, and you can't get it wrong as long as you keep writing."

"Open your writer's notebook, put today's date, and write *Hair* across the top." I keep talking, "Wherever the writing takes you, go with it. Just keep writing. The key word is *hair*." After most kids have titled their pages, I say, "On your marks. Get set. Write!"

After seven or so minutes, longer if I can get away with it, we stop writing after I say "You have one minute to come to a stopping place." We share our freewrites aloud. When students share, I always try to model pointing to something specific they did in their writing—a clear image, dialogue, humor, sentence fluency. "Reread that last sentence, Crystal."

"*I stood there, staring at the mirror, wondering if the burgundy would ever come out of my hair before the bus came,*" Crystal reads.

"Wow," I interject. "What sticks with you? What do you like about what Crystal did?" With this question students easily point out the strong bits of writing that stuck with them. They're becoming literary critics and they don't even know it. Of course, if no one can articulate a strength, I do.

The next day I read *Bedhead* again. I think repeated reading of short, engaging texts goes a long way in teaching kids what makes up good writing. By reading a text more than once, we create a shared text that we can refer to again and again—a mentor text that can show us craft and mechanics techniques. This repeated revisiting, viewing all the different layers in the text, deepens students' understanding of how to read like writers. On the second reading of *Bedhead*, I stop to demonstrate how the punctuation drives the way I read it. I type a few of the pages on transparencies. The students and I discuss what the punctuation is doing in these passages:

- Ellipses build tension.
- Short sentences and fragments fly off the tongue.
- Long sentences roll around giving us a feel for the action.

- Dialogue is between quotation marks, telling me when a person is speaking.
- Italics tell me to emphasize a word: "*Way* out of control."

Returning to our freewrites in our writer's notebooks from the day before, I direct students to play around with their text, imitating any of Palatini's punctuation or conventions. First, I model on the overhead with my freewrite. "So let's use Margie Palatini's examples to help us shape our stories. You don't have to do it just like Palatini did." I write:

> *It's midnight. I'm nervous, and my eyebrows suddenly look way too bushy.*
>
> *I pluck. No, that's not going to be fast enough. I reach for the scissors. No, I can't hold them that way and still cut. But then I see them . . . the clippers.*
>
> *Sure I have to look great to present in front of 400 teachers and the only thing standing between me and perfection are my . . . BUSHY BROWS.*
>
> *Buzz. Yes. Buzz. Yes. Buzz. Oops. No more buzz. No more middle in my left eyebrow. I stare in the mirror: one bushy brow and one half-n-half brow.*

"Play around with the punctuation in new ways." I look around the room at all of their faces. "Ask yourself what effect does it have? Go to it, and we'll share in a minute." As they start writing, I say. "Take risks. Be bold. We can always play with it more."

When students read aloud their modified freewrites, we celebrate students' use of punctuation. To do this optimally, I look at the paper as the student reads it aloud. If a teaching point happens, I write it on the board. "Look at this, Jeremy used a sentence with an introductory phrase at the beginning."

On the overhead I write, *Whenever I hear the alarm clock go off, I race to the bathroom before my sister takes it over for the next hour.* "Jeremy knew that he needed to set off sentences that start with *when* or *whenever* with a comma. Do you agree with where Jeremy inserted the comma?"

"How'd you know to put the comma after *off*, Jeremy?"

"Well, it just doesn't sound right with it someplace else." Maybe we try it in another place, maybe we rave about him using the word *race* instead of *run*. We take a few minutes to see what is right with student writing. Perhaps someone else uses a fragment effectively or adds dialogue or hyphenated adjectives. We celebrate what punctuation does, how it affects the reading of the text, and anything else well crafted. If a mistake is made, I weigh the sensitivity of the student and the importance and ease of correction. We can talk about it then or later, or ideally, I may reteach the point and have the students make their own corrections.

If I don't have time to capture all the good things a student has done, I hand out a sentence strip and a marker and ask the student to write the sentence on the strip. I can make an impromptu bulletin board titled *The Power of Punctuation*.

Of course, by processing these texts, students are going to see other valuable writer's craft techniques besides punctuation: alliteration, repetition, dialogue, and so on. That is a problem I am willing to live with in a longer lesson. I know that learning occurs at many levels in a weblike fashion, that new learning traces over itself and back again in new situations. Hearing dialogue, I may focus on the voice of it one time, and on another occasion, I may focus on the punctuation marks. Each new learning continually traces and retraces, firming up the mesh of what makes effective writing. Students literally soak up more than punctuation, and that's what I want: kids soaking up punctuation in the context of effective writing, their own and that of others.

For example, Simmy's hair story became a bit more focused with revision. She worked on correcting her spelling errors and tried to use punctuation to tell her story and break it up into chunks. She used an ellipsis to build humor and a pause at the end. She added dialogue marks when prompted by the wall chart and a re-reading of *Bedhead* (see Figure 3.3).

If you like to ride the wave of student interest, and they want more about hair, the next day you might want to continue with adding to the freewrites. For example, read *Hairs* (1997) by Sandra Cisneros. It uses sensory detail and similes with abandon in simple, elegant ways. Have students go back to their freewrites and add this kind of detail, or simply have them freewrite about their families' hair. What special effects did they create in their writing? Students can go back and add to their freewrites as many times as it's effective. In fact, they often find seeds for longer pieces.

> **Hair**
>
> My hair is so easy to put up, but I kind of got tired of my hair being so good. So, last year, when it was a hot day, I wore my black hat that said, "Not another bad hair day," and for the hair part, I teased it so it will look like I woke up on the wrong side of the bed. I went to school; all the guys were waiting for me. Everybody was in their favorite hats. I went over. "Yo, Simmy. What happened to your hair?" the guys said.
>
> "Read my hat stooges!"
>
> *Not another bad hair day.*
>
> I took off the hat, and a piece of hair was sticking up and the teased part started expanding all of a sudden. One, two, three of them started laughing. I told them I did it to make them laugh. But most of them did not believe me, even if it was true . . . or was it?

Figure 3.3 Simmy's "Hairror" Story

The Writer's Eye (I): Lists of Things I Can Write About

The "Writer's Eye (I)" section of the writer's notebook serves dual purposes:

1. Students write about the life they've observed with their own eyes, writer's eyes.
2. Students start a collection of the people, places, games, hobbies, interests, and so forth that they know well.

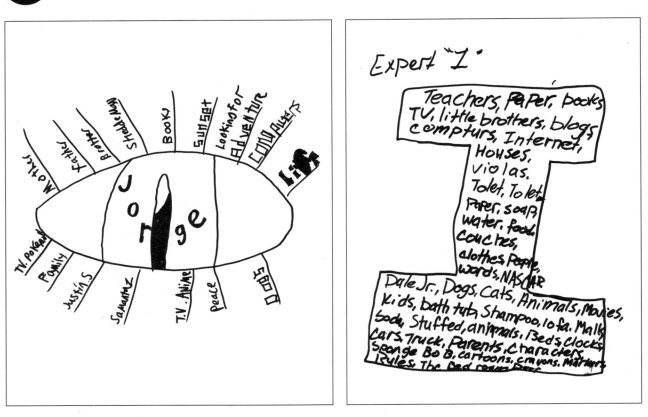

Figure 3.4 Student Writer's Eye and Writer's I
Examples

This is the space where I want to let the students know I value who they are, where they come from, and what they know. Tanesha may know a lot about her brother Roshon because she sees him every day. Roshon is part of Tanesha's life, the "I" and the "eye." So Roshon is someone who could go in Tanesha's Writer's Eye (I) list. When we tell kids to use their writer's eye, we are referring both to their noticing capabilities as well as to their personal experiences.

On the first page of the Writer's Eye (I) section of their writer's notebooks, I give students two choices of how to decorate it with words. I model both. "This graphic organizer will take up one page. You are going to list all the things in this world that you know well. This list is going to be called your Writer's Eye or Writer's I."

I show an overhead of each graphic organizer. Both have the possessive *Writer's* across the top of the page, but the *Eye* has a big *eye* drawn and each of the lashes act as a line off a web, while the *I* has a huge letter I with a fat center, providing writing space in the middle for a list (see Figure 3.4). I allow students to be creative here as long as they leave space for their lists—that's nonnegotiable.

Students draw the eye or *I* figure. I remind them again, "Make sure it takes up the whole page. You need space to write in it or around it."

Students begin the list of all the things they know: *The Simpsons,* Sony PlayStation 2, hobbies, interests, family members, friends, how to get in trouble, Math, and so on. Whether it's things at school or at home, students should list all the things they know and see most every day. Periodically, I direct students to review this list, adding and deleting as they see fit.

Craft/Mechanics Connections Through the Writer's Eye (I)

When I Was Little is my answer to all students who say, "I don't have anything to write about."

"Oh, really," I reply. *When I Was Little: A Four-Year-Old's Memoir of Her Youth* (1993) by Jamie Lee Curtis is a lively picture book that sparks memories by reflecting on eating Cheetos, naptime, floaties, and time-outs. The text follows an easy-to-imitate pattern. I read it aloud.

Afterward, I ask, "What phrase is repeated again and again?"

"When I was little," returns a chorus of voices.

"Take out your writer's notebook and turn to The Writer's Eye (I) section. Is everybody in the Writer's Eye section? Now, I want you to turn to the first empty page after your first Writer's Eye (I) list.

"On the top of the first line, I want you to write today's date. Then, skip a line and write *When I Was Little List* as the title. (I model each step on the overhead as I explain.)

"We are going to make a list of memories that all start with four words. Guess what they are?"

As the class chants, "*When I was little,*" I write the words to start my list on the overhead: *When I was little, I fell into the toilet.* "I am brainstorming by starting off everything on my list with *When I was little.*"

"Does anyone notice something else I did that we will all need to do each time on our lists?"

"You put something after it," Damien offers.

"Yes, Damien, what did I put after it?"

"That you fell in the toilet."

"Right, I put what happened when I was little. Anything else, class?" I tap on the overhead very near the comma.

"You put a comma after *little.*"

"That's right. We put a comma after *little.*" (We'll follow up with why at the end of the lesson because we need to get listing.)

"Now it's your turn. Brainstorm a list and start every memory with *When I was little.* Don't forget your comma. List as many as you can! You have four minutes—go." I continue listing on the overhead for two more entries; then

I turn off the overhead and circulate. As long as almost everybody is listing, I extend the time.

"Now tell a person near you what's on your list. You have five minutes."

After five minutes I ask, "What did you hear?" I take a few responses. "I got so many more ideas when I heard other people's lists. Let's add more to our lists. You have three minutes."

After three minutes I say, "Let's look back at our lists. Did everyone remember to use commas and to put a period at the end of each sentence? Check and fix. One minute. Go!"

"Looking over your list, do you see anything that's connected? If so, draw lines between them." I model on the overhead.

"Now go back and circle one sentence or a group of connected sentences on your list." I, of course, circle *When I was little, I fell in the toilet.*

"Turn to the first section of your writer's notebook and find the next clean page. Write today's date above the first line. Skip a line and write the title of the list: *When I Was Little.* Skip one more line and copy down the sentence or sentences you circled in the Writer's Eye (I) section. As soon as you have that down, continue freewriting for eight to ten minutes. You can't do it wrong as long as you keep writing. If you run completely dry, refer back to your list and write more. Write the entire time." Students share writing with a partner first, then a few share with the class.

I follow up with some mechanics instruction at the end of the class or first thing at the next class meeting. "So you told me I needed a comma after *When I was little,* but, at the time, I didn't ask my irritating question: Why? Why? Why do we put the comma after the *little*?"

Finally Natalie ventures a safe answer, "Because it's correct."

"Yes, it is indeed correct, Natalie, but why? Listen to me read it aloud. *When I was little* [pause], *I fell in the toilet.*"

"You paused!" Matthew blurts.

"True. The comma told me to pause. There are several words that, when they are located at the beginning of a sentence, signal you to use a comma to separate the introductory phrase from the rest of the sentence. They are comma causers."

Then, I teach students about the AAAWWUBBIS. My friend, Cathy Byrd, a sixth-grade teacher at Rudder Middle School, let me in on the power of the AAAWWUBBIS (As, Although, After, While, When, Unless, Because, Before, If, Since). The joy of this lesson comes with the AAAWWUBBIS whoop, along the lines of a good Wahoo! AAAWWUBBIS (A-WOOH-BIS)! Cathy tells her students that if they start a sentence with an AAAWWUBBIS, they are almost guaranteed to have a comma in the sentence. I remind them that the comma never immediately follows the AAAWWUBBIS. I tell them that they will hear or feel the pause when they read the sentence. I put the AAAWWUBBIS list on the board. We practice orally. The students make up a sentence beginning with an AAAWWUBBIS and tell me where they would put the comma. Later, students include at least one AAAWWUBBIS sentence in a longer piece they are working on in writer's workshop.

Later, Cathy teaches students how the AAAWWUBBIS part of the sentence is a fragment without the second part of the sentence. She says students "feel very mature when they realize how easily complex sentences can be written."

Author's Word and Phrase Palette

The "Author's Word and Phrase Palette" section of the writer's notebook will be a collection. I morphed this strategy from Noden's (1999) "Artist's Image Palette." As students read, they record words or phrases that strike them for a myriad of reasons. I wanted to open this up to a collection that could be done all year. Collecting, categorizing, and marveling at words and combinations of words in their independent and assigned reading will help students develop an appreciation for the power of words. Later, students can create a piece of writing using the palette. Students may also want to look at their palettes when revising their papers for specific word choice. In this section, students collect the following:

- *Active verbs*. Writing snaps and sizzles when active, lively verbs are used. The specificity makes writing hum with voice and often creates sounds to delight in. Active verbs like *skitter* and *crackle* should fill a lot of the space in the author's palette, developing diction and increasing vocabulary.
- *Cool words*.
- *Phrases or combinations that work*. Maybe it's alliteration, maybe it's beautiful, maybe it's parallelism, such as this sentence. For whatever reason, these word combinations dance on the page or dive into our senses, allowing us to experience whatever it is the writer is expressing.
- *Contrasts/comparisons: similes, metaphors, sensory images,* and others. I ask students to look for something fresh, not stale like "faster than a speeding bullet," but new, original, and something to aspire to as a writer: [*This cake*] *tastes like vacuum cleaner fuzz* (Korman 2000, p. 2) or *Her open eye was like nearly black balsamic vinegar beading on white china* (Franzen 2001, p. 31). While reading *Birdland* by Tracy Mack (2003), I recorded these similes in my author's palette: *Her voice was rough, like a bus grinding its brakes* (p. 36) and *Leo's feet pad down the hallway like a soft drumbeat* (p. 66). While reading *The Truth About Sparrows* by Marian Hale (2004), I copied, *Sweat crawled all over me like ants* (p. 2). Whatever strikes me for whatever reason, I record it. I ask my students to do the

The Kite Runner by Khaled Hosseini	
Active Verbs	**Smart Similes**
peeking claws sparkled propelled glanced soared floating giggling mumble hand picked slung	*. . . a face like a* *Chinese doll chiseled* *from hardwood: his flat,* *broad nose and* *slanting, narrow eyes* *like bamboo leaves . . .* (p. 3) *Hassan never talked* *about his mother, as if* *she'd never existed.* (p. 6)
Naming Names (Specific Nouns)	**Awesome Adjectives**
receiver Golden Gate Park alley afterthought chandelier	frigid meaty slanting affluent grainy *wrought-iron* gates *intricate* mosaic tiles *sprawling* house *vaulted* ceiling *mahogany* table *paper-thin* layer of muscle *scraggly* legs

Figure 3.5 Teacher Model of Author's Word Palette

same. Noden (1999) suggests that we can use authors' words and phases to inspire us to paint our words in our own writing.

For example, as I read *The Kite Runner* by Khaled Hosseini (2003), I jotted down words and organized them into four categories. I placed the categories in the four quadrants of my author's palette and labeled the quadrants with the types of words I had found (see Figure 3.5). Categories can morph. I might have a list of how characters move, and so on. Later, kids return to this list and dip their pencils in the words and phrases and place them in their own writing. By categorizing words, we have a concrete way to stay in touch with parts of speech, emphasize function, and work on the writer's craft of word choice.

Gems: Sentences and Paragraphs that Work

To distinguish the Author's Palette from the "Gems" section of the writer's notebook (Thomas 2000, Harwayne 1992), I tell students that "gems" will always be full sentences or more.

Instead of phrases or words that resonate with the reader, for this section I want students to hunt down sentences that work, strings of sentences, even paragraphs that make the reader stop, bend over, pick up the gem and see it sparkle in the light from many angles. Gems make us pause and say, "How'd they do that?" By having them in a collection, writers can return to these gems and enjoy them again and again—a treasure trove of fluent, fierce writing worth a second look, worth imitating.

Because students choose what they like, this is much less a lesson in grammar or style than a lesson in art appreciation and collection. I ask students to dedicate one page of their writer's notebook to sentences with introductory phrases, one page to sentences with interrupting phrases, and one to those with closing phrases. This way the kids focus on the patterns rather than the labels, increasing the likelihood that the students will own these complex sentence structures and find them seeping into their writing, spilling over from the stores of good writing they are immersing themselves in. For younger or less experienced writers, it may be easier to have students record their sentences on strips of typing paper that you have pre-cut. That way the kids can have more support when categorizing them. If a student gets stuck, I ask the class to help figure out which category the sentence fits in, while mediating the discussion with questions.

Of course, some sentences will fit in more than one category—a "combination platter," if you will. When faced with this choice, students can highlight the part of the sentence they want to emphasize or make a new category altogether. See Figure 3.6 for an example of a combination platter and its choice for categorization.

Becoming More Intentional with Sentence Pattern Collections

When I want to make the sentence patterns more explicit, I give students inserts for their writer's notebooks that have the general information about a pattern and some correct examples to start with. I found that when I had students copy down patterns from the overhead, sometimes errors were made and then they were being scaffolded with wrong information until I caught it in their notebooks. I found that creating the inserts with patterns, such as participles, prepositions, and absolutes, gives me a treasure trove of stylistic and grammatical devices that I can pull out at a moment's notice. At the beginning of the year, I run off all the patterns (templates for these cards are included in the Appendix). Then I cut them up into half pages and paper clip each one until I need it.

Once we look at some sentences that have -ing verbs and we start playing around with the structure, I can hand out the Comma Reinforcers on participles, and kids can glue them into their writer's notebooks at the top of a page. Beneath these headers, kids can collect samples from their favorite authors and other students, or in many cases from their own writing. See the Appendix and the lessons on individual devices in Part II for more information.

A Combination Platter Served by Judy Moody

AAAWWWUBBIS/Opener

While she munched, Judy watched her little brother, Stink, hang stuff up on the refrigerator: his report card, the self portrait that made him look like a monkey, and a photo of himself in his flag costume, from the time he went to Washington D.C. without her.

Appositive/Interrupter

While she munched, Judy watched her little brother, **Stink,** hang stuff up on the refrigerator: his report card, the self portrait that made him look like a monkey, and a photo of himself in his flag costume, from the time he went to Washington D.C. without her.

Commas in a Series/Closer

While she munched, Judy watched her little brother, Stink, hang stuff up on the refrigerator: **his report card, the self portrait that made him look like a monkey, and a photo of himself in his flag costume, from the time he went to Washington D.C. without her.**

—Megan McDonald, *Judy Moody Gets Famous!* (pp. 13–14)

Figure 3.6 A Combination Platter

More Writer's Notebook Tips

Here are some additional tips for handling and storing writer's notebooks as well as some excellent models and resources from which to garner more ideas.

Handling the Notebooks

- *Do they go home?* I choose to leave the notebooks in the classroom, but if for any reason a notebook is missing, I allow the student to do the work and then glue it in the proper place in the writer's notebook later.
- *Storage?* To keep each class's notebooks organized, I have colored crates, labeled for each class. Some years I have had shelf space and then I use that.
- *What if they mess up?* If a big mistake happens in the notebook and it must be corrected or covered, glue a sheet, cut to fit, over the mistake. "Everything is fixable, except tearing out pages!"

Models of Keeping Notebooks

Berne, Suzanne. *A Crime in the Neighborhood.*
Byrd, Robert. *Leonardo: Beautiful Dreamer.*
Haddix, Margaret Peterson. *Don't You Dare Read This, Mrs. Dunphrey.*
Moss, Marissa. *Max's Logbook.*
Moss, Marissa. *Amelia's Notebook.*
Moss, Marissa. *My Notebook (with Help from Amelia).*
Schotter, Roni. *Nothing Ever Happens on 90th Street.*

Resources for Writer's Notebooks

Buckner, Aimee. *Notebook Know-How.*
Bomer, Randy. *Time for Meaning.*
Fletcher, Ralph. *A Writer's Notebook.*
Fletcher, Ralph. *Breathing In, Breathing Out: Keeping a Writer's Notebook.*
Goldberg, Natalie. *Writing Down the Bones.*

Okay, about now, you're probably saying, "Wait a minute, what about the grammar and mechanics in the writer's notebook? With all this free movement, weaving, discovery, context, collections, and dancing around in the messiness of real writing, how do I systematize what I'm teaching? Where do I hold all this freewheeling knowledge, and how on earth can I ground this knowledge long enough to be etched in my students' individual repertoires?" All I have done so far is discuss how to construct the playground. The editor's checklist is my tool for helping students become systematic in integrating mechanics growth into their writing.

Starting an Editor's Checklist

Because I want to be a responsive teacher, responding to my students' grammatical and mechanical needs as they arise, I have to strike a balance between what students may need at any given time and the overall blueprint of what my kids should know and be able to do when they walk out of my class at the end of the year. The editor's checklist is an essential tool for meeting this goal in my classroom. This one tool can serve as a blueprint for the year, a placeholder, a record of your grammar and mechanics teaching.

I don't mean the editor's checklist found at the teacher supply store, or the lengthy list that comes with textbooks, or even the individual list that your students *don't* keep in their writing folders.

I bow down to worship any teacher who can get all of his or her students to keep their own personalized lists of idiosyncratic errors, but *I* could only keep up with these individualized checklists with my 150 students for about three weeks into the semester. I stress the word *I* because if I did not sit with individual students and tell them what they needed to work on, the lists were never made or added to or even referred to. It's just like when I corrected errors on their papers. I would hope that if I sit next to them, working one-on-one, they would learn new writing skills by my modeling.

Researchers tell us to teach skills in context. They tell us to conference for one-on-one instruction, but I had thirty other students who were clamoring for me to assist them as well. I wonder, do math teachers teach most skills one-on-one? These attempts at teaching mechanics didn't work because I never got to every kid. And I just deepened their dependence on some "other" authority instead of scaffolding them to tackle and reason with grammar and mechanics on their own.

Finally, I began keeping an organic editor's checklist: a system that grows from student writing and what research says kids have to know. In my class, we constantly move back and forth between the editor's checklist and writer's notebook.

On the first day of school, I hang a long piece of white butcher paper on the wall, in a spot everyone can see. If kids ask about it, I tell them this sheet is going to help them grow up and be ready for high school. If no one says anything, I say, "So when are y'all going to leave me alone about the white butcher paper?" I get puzzled looks. I love to puzzle my kids. I tell them their brains are growing.

On the second day, before school, I write across the top in big green letters *Editor's Checklist.*

"I think you are now ready for me to share with you," I say, pointing at the butcher paper, "the editor's checklist."

Audible groan. Just the word *editing* sends shivers down students' spines. Who can blame them? Especially when they are assuming it is probably just one more way to make writing like filling out a worksheet. Their adolescent brains downshift: One more way to be wrong; one more rule that doesn't make sense and doesn't apply to me; one more thing I couldn't care less about; one more thing to check off, be done with, so I can sit, talk, and write notes. When I have given my students a photocopied checklist in the past, that is, in fact, what they have done. They have checked off each box, one at a time. Checklists mostly get us checks, not editing, but this organic editor's checklist is different.

"Have you ever seen an editor's checklist?" Most students say no, even though they probably have seen one in one form or another. "This chart is going to help us learn many of the important things to be adult writers. Writers' secrets, if you will." A good percentage of my middle school students want to be adults, so I shamelessly use this desire to manipulate them into caring about mechanics. "You're not a child anymore," I say, "but you're not an adult either. You're in between. One of the ways we make our writing more adult is to use punctuation marks correctly." I get a few smirks, but I have everyone's attention.

"Have you ever thought about why we have punctuation? Or better yet, why we have laws and rules everywhere we go?"

"So we won't get in trouble," offers Stephanie.

"Tell me more, Stephanie."

"Well, it's like we can't go through stop signs because there would be a crash."

"What other rules keep you safe?"

Albert's hand shoots up. "The pool over at San Pedro Park; there are these signs that say 'No Running.'"

"At Pecan Grove Apartments it says the same thing," adds Ramiro.

"Can anyone think of a pool where they want you to run?" I ask.

Silence envelops the room as they search their brains.

"I guess that rule is pretty standard." We talk about the conventions of eating at the table, restaurants, driving. After we have exhausted all the possible places where rules serve us, I ask, "Whom do you think invented conventions or rules for writing?"

"Teachers?" wonders Jeremy.

"Maybe there was this mean English teacher a long time ago who had a red pen for a hand," I say, holding my right arm stiff in front of me, thrashing it around in crossing-out motions. "And she just started marking up papers for fun, slashing them to bits."

"Whatever!" Sara says.

"No, it wasn't a mean old teacher with a red-pen hand. It was the writers. They wanted to be understood. Don't you want to be understood too? Grammar and mechanics are conventions. The word *convention* meant *agreement* in its original Latin form. You told me we had agreements or rules about eating, being at a pool, and so on. You said they told us how to act. Well, writers wanted people to understand what they said, even when they weren't around. They wanted people to understand their words so they started agreeing on things: A period means stop this thought; a capital letter signals that a new sentence is beginning or that a word is a name."

This discussion begins building the concept. Referring to the editor's checklist, I explain how we will learn more about how to follow the rules and how following conventions of mechanics and grammar makes our writing easier to understand. And what middle school students want is to be understood—finally.

"Are you tired of nobody hearing you? Writing gives you that power, and part of writing's power is in its passion, its details, but all of that is lost if the grammar and mechanics can't hold the message together."

Soon after, I read *Punctuation Takes a Vacation*. This whimsical picture book by Robin Pulver (2003) describes the plight of a class whose punctuation gets so sick and tired of being erased, left out, and moved around that all the punctuation marks rebel and go on vacation. The story and illustrations describe how much punctuation is missed. The book is one more way to stress the value of punctuation as a tool writers harness to communicate.

Where Do I Begin My Editor's Checklist?

In truth, the editor's checklist may only be semiorganic. While it grows from the hubris of student writing, it also incorporates my state standards along with Connors and Lunsford's top twenty errors, listed in Chapter 1.

Figure 3.7 Editor's Checklist Wall Chart

After I teach grammar and mechanics concepts through snippets of text or writers' secrets, students help me list each rule on the editor's checklist (see Figure 3.7). If appropriate, we add an annotation that reminds them of how to apply the rule and its purpose. It may be more appropriate to refer to another list posted in the room or to start a different wall chart. Figure 3.8 offers advice about which rules could go on the editor's checklist and which could be posted separately. I find that posting capitalization rules and sentence patterns by themselves has several advantages. Separate lists serve as categorical organization for the high-priority rules and ensure that there is room left on the editor's checklist for other important rules.

The First Entry

At the beginning of the year, students complete form after form and label after label. One of the most useful rules to introduce at the beginning of the year is capitalization. I lit on capitalization to start my editor's checklist because (1) its use is immediate,

What Could Go on the Editor's Checklist?

What Could Go on the List?	What Could Get Its Own List?
Check capitalization	Capitalization
Check homophones	Word wall of homophones and frequently misspelled words
Check commas	
Check pronouns	Compound sentence patterns
Check apostrophes	
Check subject-verb agreement	Complex sentence patterns
Check double negatives	Serial comma patterns
Check dialogue	Pronouns
	Two-word sentences
	Verb tense
	Dialogue rules

Figure 3.8 What Could Go on the Editor's Checklist?

Capitalization Rules!

1. Proper nouns
   (**R**ayburn **M**iddle **S**chool, **S**an **A**ntonio, **B**rittany)
2. Proper Adjectives
   (**E**nglish muffin, **S**ony television, **C**hinese food)
3. Title with a last name
   (**C**oach **A**nderson, **P**resident **L**incoln)
4. First word in a direct quotation
   (**V**anessa asked, "**W**hat can I write about?")
5. Titles
   (*The Giver*, *Seventeen*, *King of the Hill*)
6. Letter opening
   (**D**ear **M**r. **C**hips,)
7. First word of a letter closing
   (**Y**ours truly,)

Figure 3.9 Capitalization Rules!

and (2) the rules of capitalization are black and white and straightforward. Why start with something riddled with exceptions?

This way I can lull kids into believing that this grammar thing isn't so far out of reach.

I introduce the seven capitalization rules over several days by having students look at and create examples in the context of sentences, check their own work as well as others', and create a mini-rule book to keep in their writing folders. I then post the capitalization rules (see Figure 3.9).

Once the rules are understood, we are ready to be held accountable for capitalization. I walk over to the editor's checklist. "It's time for our first entry on our growing list of things to edit in our writing. From now on, every time you finish a piece of writing, instead of saying, 'I'm finished,' I want you to look at this list and reread your work, correcting it for capitalization." I write *Check capitalization* beneath the header *Editor's Checklist*. For other rules, we might make an annotation at the bottom of the list with key ideas to help spark our memories, but our high-priority capitalization rules have a separate poster. I remind kids that if they need more information, they can look at the capitalization poster.

Once we have zoomed in on a rule, how do we zoom back out? We go from looking at sentences to looking at paragraphs of our own writing and that of our peers. This needs to be a quick process, one that's easy and can be repeated with many mechanics concepts—if we're ever going to get those concepts in front of them enough, if we're ever going to get them to care and to know what to care about.

Express-Lane Edits: Returning to Context

One thing all my students are familiar with is the express lane at the grocery store. Sometimes you don't have time to shop for everything. If you only need to get a carton of milk, you can go through the express lane and save time and hassle. I try to take this familiar part of our weekly routines and merge it into editing tasks.

How often do we get bogged down in the totality of all that needs fixing so that editing becomes an ordeal for students as well as the teacher? What if we narrowed down our editing task to a few items? We'd be able to edit more often and more quickly and to make editing in context more a part of the everyday fabric of writer's workshop. In short, "express-lane edits" get my students rereading their work and thinking about how to edit their writing in ways that clarify their ideas. It is also my version of "Clean up on aisle 3!" It helps us focus on that editor's check-list, moving the principles into the writer's notebook. I can post anything on my classroom walls, but if I don't use it, my students won't, and they won't inter-nalize the concepts.

Each student needs a piece of first-draft writing to begin—not a final copy or a completed essay, but a messy beginning like a writer's notebook entry or a freewrite. I use freewrites to get my students writing fluently; I use express-lane edits to get my students editing fluently.

First, as with most things, I model the process I want them to engage in. While students freewrite, I write an entry on a transparency. After the free-write, I say, "I know many of you go to the store a lot. When you're in a hurry, which line do you go to?"

"The express lane."

"It's quick. You're in, you're out," I add. I explain that, like the routine they are used to at the store, I want them to become equally familiar with using express-lane edit as a way to reread their writing, a way to "check out" important items in their work.

"For example, we've been talking about apostrophes—when to insert and when to delete them. I want to show you a quick way to deal with this editing item. I call it the express-lane edit."

I turn the overhead on, revealing my freewrite (see Figure 3.10). "Let's take the freewrite we did on neighbors," I say. "Now, before I read it, I need to make my shopping list." Beneath my writing, on the left half of the trans-parency I draw a box.

"We have to decide what's going to go in the box—a sort of shopping list." I write *Items to "Check Out"* at the top of the box (see Figure 3.10).

Neighbor Freewrite—Express-Lane Edit Example

When I was five, I wished our neighbor, Mrs. Harrison, were my mother. I wanted to ride around Nederland in Mrs. Harrisons Ford LTD station wagon. It's sides had wood panels and the station wagon's cargo area in back had a trundle seat that pulled up from the floor and made a bench. I coveted that sunken bench, forest green with its own tiny push button seatbelt.

Mom's car was just a boring Plymouth—no wood panels, no trundle seat, no Mrs. Harrison with her sweet perfume and frosted blonde hair. Just our plain old Plymouth and my plain old Mom who smelled like cigarettes and Jergen's hand lotion. She's never going to be like the other Moms, I remember thinking to myself.

Items to "Check Out"	Receipt
• Apostrophes Use apostrophes to show ownership except with pronouns (hers, its) Only use apostrophes with pronouns if you are making a contraction (he's = he is, it's = it is) • Capitalization	I changed *Harrisons* to *Harrison's* by inserting an apostrophe because the *apostrophe s* shows it was *Mrs. Harrison's LTD*. I changed *it's* to *its* because *it's = it is*, and I meant ownership. Don't use apostrophes with pronouns unless you want a contraction!

Figure 3.10 Neighbor Freewrite—Express-Lane Edit Example

Think-Aloud Example

The Writing on the Overhead	What I Say Aloud to Show My Thinking Process
When I was five, I wished our neighbor, Mrs. Harrison, ~~were~~ my mother. I wanted to ride around Nederland in Mrs. **Harrisons** Ford LTD station wagon. **It's** sides had wood panels and the station wagon's cargo area in back had a trundle seat that pulled up from the floor and made a seat. I coveted that forest green seat, with its own tiny seatbelt. Mom's car was just a boring Plymouth—no wood panels . . .	"Okay, I see that I was trying to show whose Ford it was, and we use apostrophes to show ownership. So I need to change *Harrisons* to *Harrison's*, adding an apostrophe. Now I need to write that in my receipt box." "I see another apostrophe on *it's*. I know people always make mistakes with *it's* so I need to really think about this. An apostrophe shows ownership, but wait. (I walk over to my wall chart on apostrophes.) That's right, they can show contractions, too. And *it's* means *it is*. I don't mean that here. I am not saying 'It is sides.' (I point to the poster.) That's right. Never use apostrophes with possessive pronouns. Apostrophes with pronouns mean contractions, never possession. I need to write this change in my receipt box." [I also think aloud about the other apostrophes as well, letting students tell me why they are correct or incorrect.]

Figure 3.11 Think-Aloud Example

"Since we just added apostrophes to our editor's checklist, let's 'check out' our freewrites for apostrophes. Should we insert or delete any?" I write *apostrophes* in my box. Students copy the box, title, and word *apostrophes* beneath their freewrites in their writer's notebooks. This is the perfect time for a quick review; I have students copy a few details about apostrophes that we have been discussing (see Figure 3.10). Next, we draw another box to the right of the *Items to "Check Out"* box. "The box on the right is titled *Receipts*. In this box, you show me your changes."

"Now we're ready to do the express-lane edit. Before you try, I will show you how to do it using my writing." I read over the text, making my invisible thinking process visible by thinking aloud—modeling my problem-solving process. Figure 3.11 shows some "think-aloud" comments I make while modeling.

As I make changes, I add each change to my "Receipts" box. I model using the language our state test uses, including *insert* and *delete*. Then I have students do the express-lane edit on their own writing. If they find nothing to change, they read it a second time. If students still find no mistakes, they read the writing backwards, word by word, like some journalists do. If they find nothing at all to correct, they write *I found no errors after reading the above writing three times*, followed by their signature. This way everyone always has a receipt.

As an extension, I may cue students to use a specific convention or grammatical construction before they begin their freewrite. Then whatever they were cued to use will be our focus in the express-lane edit.

While the students reread their work for the express-lane edit, I like to play music. A perfect piece for this is "The Typewriter" by Leonard Slatkin, which is easily and inexpensively available on the iTunes Web site. Music does much to change the affect of these mechanics-rich experiences.

If students are only rereading their work, we are making a step in the right direction. What's really funny is that kids, when limited to what they should edit, for some reason love to edit for something you didn't list. "Sir, I spelled a word wrong. Can I fix that?" I respond, as if I am doing them a favor, "Well, I guess." Again, if the only benefit they get from this is rereading, then that's a start. And, if I am calling their attention to an important concept in a real context, that's even better. If they actually integrate an apostrophe consciousness into their rereading and rechecking process, Hallelujah! That's the goal.

The express-lane edit is a class ritual that can be done with or without partners and gives us the ever-important repetition in a meaningful context.

Comma Reinforcers: Cut-and-Paste Mini-Handbooks for the Writer's Notebook

Because the comma is the most used punctuation mark (Connors and Lunsford 1997), I have found that commas need to be reinforced more than any other punctuation mark. I developed comma mini-handbooks called "comma reinforcers" that can be pasted into the writer's notebooks one pattern at a time. In the Appendix, there are six comma patterns with the support of student-friendly definitions and examples from literature. These include comma patterns for participles, absolutes, appositives, adjectives out of order, subordinating conjunctions (AAAWWUBBIS), and prepositional phrases. (See Figure 3.12 for an example of the participle comma reinforcer. It shows one of the comma reinforcers found in the Appendix. Each pattern can be pasted in the writer's notebooks for additional reinforcement of commas.)

I like to photocopy all of the comma reinforcers at the beginning of the year. I cut them into individual patterns and paper clip each stack together until I need to use one of them in class to support writers. I then have ready-to-go comma reinforcers. Kids paste them into their notebooks. They work well at the top of each page of collections in the

Figure 3.12 Cut-and-Paste Comma Reinforcers

Use Comma(s)

Participles

Participles and participial phrases are *-ing* verbs and *-ed* verbs that evoke action and movement in our sentences, either to start a phrase or have a series. (Participles can be *-en* verbs, too.)

Wishing *it were cooler and wishing she weren't hungry,* Franny Davis stood in line at the school cafeteria door, **fingering *the lunch pass in her pocket.*** (p. 1)
—Mary Stolz, *The Noonday Friends*

The bus motor idles, **putting *out a long tornado of blue smoke.*** (p. 6)
—Chuck Palahniuk, *Choke*

Burping, growing, throwing, running—*everything is a race.* (p. 6)
—Jerry Spinelli, *Loser*

"Gems" section of the writer's notebook, making sure that kids have correct information at their fingertips for easy reference. I like my kids to keep collections of stunning sentences that can fit under each pattern.

In the Appendix, I have also included many other mini-handbook entries that can be cut and pasted into the writer's notebook whenever writers need extra support. Not every student will become fluent with every pattern. But each student will have support, a reference, and a place to play, collect, and experiment with grammar and mechanics. Gluing these tools right into the middle of the writer's notebook means inserting them directly into the context of daily writing.

Off-the-Wall Grammar and Mechanics Instruction

Picture in your mind's eye a classroom with almost every inch of wall space covered with sheets of long butcher paper hanging vertically—some white, some yellow, all messy with examples written in marker. You see titles such as "Editor's Checklist" and "Leads that Make You Want to Read." Right beside these, another chart states a comma rule. Beneath the comma rule are example after example of the comma rule in sentences from the literature of Robert Cormier to Roberto from third period. Meaningful print is every-where. It looks like Strunk and White's *Elements of Style* exploded on the classroom walls.

There are no prefab, purchased posters and wall charts—only organic, growing, changing charts that address what kids need to know to survive in the world of writing. And these wall charts are used, referred to, pointed at, moved, and looked at. These wall charts are a living part of my class's meaning-making journey.

Mechanics are a visual skill. Kids have to "see" mechanics in action to absorb the patterns and use them. Requisite rules and examples must be in front of students' faces when they need clarification and stylistic options in the midst of the writing process. And mechanics and craft connections have to be seen repeatedly. Mechanics are meant to serve the writer in meaning-making; however, to correctly use these tools, young writers must know their options and what those options look like in various contexts. Why not cover our rooms with the examples, rules, and charts? Wall charts are more than decoration; they're brain magic.

Brain researchers Renata and Geoffrey Caine (1994) prescribe that learning should be "a combination of spontaneity and design" (p. 2). These organic wall charts are just that. They grow from my students' meaning-making. Before I make a wall chart, I ask myself the following:

51

- What do my students need in order to communicate their thinking?
- What effects are they trying to create as writers?
- What craft would help students more fully express themselves in writing?
- What are the "big-ticket" items? (The grammar and mechanics rules that mean the most—have the highest payoff.)
- How much context can I include and still have the poster be visible from a distance?

Since the brain searches for patterns, it is the English teacher's job to expose students to stylistic and syntactic options multiple times, in multiple ways, to constantly expand what and how our kids "see."

Addressing specifically the need for visuals, Caine and Caine state, "Learning involves both focused and peripheral perceptions" (1994, p. 91). So this stuff on the walls works even when our students are staring at the wall instead of us. A pattern is being visually imprinted.

Dallas Lozada, a seventh-grade teacher whom I coached, said, "Even after I took the wall charts down for the state test, the kids would look on the walls where they hung and could still see them in their minds." Her passing rate went up 13 percent after her first year of using wall charts. "Wall charts helped the kids finally get the rules, even memorize some of them."

Elementary teachers have always known the power of a humble piece of butcher paper and an accessible marker. Word lists and processes cover the walls of most elementary classrooms. When I started teaching middle school, my goal was to use this tried-and-true technique of elementary teachers with more complex information. Not just lists, but the rules or principles middle school students need to know. Elementary teachers also harness the power of including students' ideas on wall charts. Middle school students have the motor skills to actually write their own contributions, and they are still thrilled to see their ideas on the walls.

There is a difference between wall charts and posters. Wall charts are made of butcher paper and should have room at the bottom to add examples and new rules. Posters contain more set information that won't necessarily grow. Wall charts never get finished; posters do. For students, wall charts serve multiple purposes. The charts:

- Act as a visual cue
- Provide a scaffold for complex information
- Immerse students in multiple models
- Guide students in categorizing and organizing information
- Remind students which rules really count

Students aren't the only ones who benefit from wall charts. For those of us who feel less confident with rules, they are right there on the wall and don't always have to be recalled in our heads. Wall charts also:

- *Provide easy access to examples and rules.* When the class encounters an example of a rule in literature or a problem in creating a text, you have a ready-made visual to highlight, revisit, or add to.
- *Teach when you're busy with other students.* Students don't have to ask you the question. Instead of "Look it up," I can say, "Look on the wall." If I don't have the needed wall chart, I make a note to create the needed chart in an upcoming lesson. When I see an error on a student paper, I ask students to look at the sentence again. If they don't catch their error, I say, "Look over here." I tap on the wall chart.

Figure 4.1 Student Writes on a Sentence Strip to Add to a Wall Chart

"Does this help? Can you see how you can use this pattern in that sentence? Let me see what you come up with. Maybe we'll add it to the wall." With this continual reference to the walls, students will refer themselves and each other to the stylebook that your classroom walls have become.
- *Anchor everyone in crucial content.* Teachers are constantly pulled in every direction and increasingly are held responsible for teaching more and more information. Well-selected wall charts can anchor you to what's important, to what you need to revisit, and to what content you should be addressing.
- *Are living organisms.* Because wall charts are based on student need and high-payoff mechanics, they grow throughout the year. They are novel, but ritualistic. Since they include kids' ideas and their personally selected examples from literature, the students value these charts. Since they grow, kids take responsibility for the charts. The wall charts belong to the class and breathe life into it whenever they are used.

Working with Wall Charts: A Classroom Snapshot

Since I know my students learn skills better when they are mapped into a whole, before designing any mechanics or craft lesson that will involve a wall chart, I consider two things:

- What are my students writing now?
- What skills do they need to effectively achieve that purpose?

For example, when my students are writing narratives in writer's workshop, I teach the conventions of dialogue. I've never met a batch of middle school students who could correctly punctuate dialogue. Many have never noticed the conventions that they have become accustomed to as readers.

The first place I look to teach kids about writing is on the bookshelves. Jack Gantos's novel *Heads or Tails: Stories from the Sixth Grade* (1995) has an early passage that students can easily relate to. Not only do I use it to teach dialogue, but I also use it to spark a freewrite in which students can apply the rules they are hopefully learning.

"Have you ever had a fight with your brother or sister?" I ask. Hands shoot up. "How about a friend you spent too much time with?" More hands.

"How many of you have brothers or sisters? What do you fight over?"

After eliciting several responses from the point of view of big and little siblings, I introduce the book and read the following passage aloud.

> *This evening would be no different. Without writing much of anything, I locked my diary, grabbed a deck of cards and fled my bedroom. Betsy was sitting at the dining room table playing a hand of solitaire. I sat down across from her and began to lie out my cards.*
>
> *"Stop that," she said sharply.*
>
> *"What?" I said.*
>
> *"Stop copying me," she said. "Mom, tell him to stop copying me. He's driving me crazy."*
>
> *"Leave your sister alone," Mom said, "and come help me work on this jigsaw puzzle. I'm having trouble."*
>
> *Betsy slapped her cards down on the table. "Don't let him help you, Mom," she said. "Make him think of something to do on his own. Everything I do, he wants to do. Everything you do, he wants to do. He doesn't have a brain in his head. He's like some kind of dumb animal. Monkey see, monkey do."*
>
> *"That's enough," Mom said. But we knew Betsy was right. I couldn't come up with any great ideas on my own. Nothing interested me until I saw another person do it first. (pp. 5–6)*

I look up from the book and take a breath, "What did you notice?"

Joseph says, squinting his eyes, "That sounds like my little brother."

"So you and your brother have sibling rivalry," I say, writing the words *sibling rivalry* on the board.

"Yeah, I guess, if that means we fight over the TV remote," Joseph adds.

"That's exactly what it means." I turn back to the class, "Did this remind anybody else of their brothers or sisters, big or little?"

Pricilla says, "It sounds more like me and Lettie."

"You and your friend Lettie argue. About what?" The discussion continues. "Does anyone want to see what this passage looks like on the page?" I put the excerpt on the overhead, enlarged so everyone can see it.

"Does anybody notice anything about punctuation or conventions?"

"When people talk they have those thingies around what they say." Charles curls two fingers on each hand.

"Yes, Charles." Smiling, I ask, "Does anybody remember what we call those two . . . *thingies*?"

"Dialogue!" Jeremy blurts out, eager to please.

As always, discussions about mechanics may take a while, but this discussion proceeds meaningfully, and when it doesn't, I lead. While discussing what students notice, I point to the different text features on the overhead. "Right, Jeremy, the thingies do indicate there is dialogue, but we have another name for the thingies."

Finally someone says *quotation marks*. I write *quotation marks* on the board and circle the punctuation marks on the overhead, asking someone to read what comes between them. As the class looks at the model, I keep asking them, "What else do you notice? What else?" And eventually, students address all the dialogue conventions, or I point them out. We can list several points on the board that we can also circle in the example.

"How can you tell when each person is talking?"

Jessica points out, "With the *saids*. The *saids* tell you who's talking."

"Okay, the *saids*. Does anyone know the fancy high school word for the *said Betsy* or *said Mom*?" This is a good time to teach the term *attribution*. "Now look here. I can tell Betsy is speaking because it has that 'said thing,' as Jessica calls it, or what else is that called?"

"*Attribution*."

"But what about this next line?" Chris notices that when Jack speaks next, the line is indented. "Does anyone have a theory for why it's indented?" I listen to different answers.

"Maybe it's like a new paragraph," Jessica offers.

"Right, Jess, it is a new paragraph because it is indented. Let's look again." I point to the first few lines of dialogue. "Why do you think it's indented?"

"The first one says she said it and the next one says I said it. Then she said it again." Jessica says with a new sureness, "They do it every time somebody says something."

"Let's look at the rest and check out the theory." After going through the passage and seeing that Gantos indeed indents a line every time a new person speaks, I extract an answer from the group, guiding them until we invent a statement such as *Indent every time a new person speaks*. I write the statement or rule on the board under the heading *Dialogue Rules!*

Because no one notices that each quote starts with a capital letter, I walk over to the *Capitalization Rules!* poster I've had up since the first day of school. "Hmm, I wonder if there's help anywhere in the room?" Looking directly at the poster, I say, "I wonder where." Hands shoot up, and Justine reads the rule. I add it to our growing list of dialogue conventions on the board: *Capitalize the first word in a direct quotation.* Our conversation continues until we exhaust all the comma conventions (and some of the students as well).

Watching Sergio yawn, I wouldn't dream of having the students copy the *Dialogue Rules!* chart (see Figure 4.2) into their writer's notebooks. Not yet. I will do it tomorrow—another opportunity for repetition, with the wall chart and the writer's notebook reinforcing each other.

Next we reread the passage to see how the rules look in motion, noting all the rules in context on the overhead. Then, students freewrite on sibling rivalry, attempting to use as much dialogue correctly as possible—approximating, using, looking back at the rules or examples, internalizing. I notice some kids looking at the model on the overhead for imitation. Then we share with a partner and write again, because students have more ideas they want to get down before they forget.

After school I whip out my markers and memorialize our thinking on a piece of butcher paper, so we can use the board again tomorrow.

The next day, students copy the cleaned-up dialogue rules into the writers' secrets section of their writer's notebook. The students will use those rules to complete an express-lane edit of their sibling rivalry freewrites, noting what is correct and which rules they still need to work on.

"Raise your hand if you found an error in your writing."

Adrianna raises her hand, still looking at her writing.

"What mistake did you find, Adrianna?"

"I didn't close my thingies."

"Your quotation marks?"

"Yeah, I put 'em at the beginning, but I didn't at the end." Other students quickly look over their writing again.

"Did anyone else find that mistake? As an old teacher, I have seen plenty of middle school students forget to close their quotes."

Students put away their sibling rivalry pieces, open their writing folders and take out whatever drafts they plan to work on in writer's workshop. "When you reread your writing, you may find a place where dialogue could add to your story, essay, or poem. When you're finished, you can edit for correct use against our new *Dialogue Rules!* chart posted on the wall." In this way, students play around with the concept of dialogue and the signals it sends readers in their own writing. Now that I have explicitly taught dialogue in the context of reading and writing, I layer the concept into our daily work by pointing it out in our reading and referring back to it in our drafting, revising, and editing phases.

Throughout the year I return to the posted rules, pointing them out, asking students why the writer made this choice or that and what those choices communicate.

Figure 4.2 Dialogue Rules!

The point is, visuals help fit grammar and mechanics issues into the whole of our teaching, by showing the skills and strategies writers authentically need to communicate their thinking. And sometimes we give them information about punctuation or stylistic tools they wouldn't have ever imagined they needed.

Wall Charts That Work

What makes a wall chart work? Content? Size? Placement? All these things and more. Over the years, I have experimented with many variables and have found what works best. To ensure an optimal experience with wall charts, I have honed a few guidelines:

- *Write big.* Write in letters large enough to be read easily from anywhere in the classroom.
- *Include examples.* Examples from literature and student writing put rules in a meaningful context and serve as models.
- *Use color.* Highlight crucial information or draw attention to a particular place with bright colors or highlighters.

- *Use light backgrounds.* As a general rule, use butcher paper or posters with light backgrounds. This creates enough contrast so that the words can be read.
- *Place carefully.* It all depends on your room, but place similar rules together. I always have a comma corner and a consistent place for my editor's checklist. If I am going to need to write on this poster, I consider: Can I reach it? Can they see it? Can I write on it?
- *Have students use sentence strips.* Even though their motor skills have grown, I have found that kids do better when I hand them a sentence strip to use for adding materials to wall charts with more text. Students can stabilize the strip and write on a flat surface, using the unlined side. If they need more space, they can tape two sentence strips together. Middle school students have trouble writing on the wall, and the sentence strip has the added benefit of containing students' writing in a specified space. Using a sentence strip also allows more than one kid to write a contribution for a chart at the same time. Plus, it is easier to correct a sentence strip than a mistake on a huge chart.

If you can't write in a way that others can read, find a student or colleague who can. You can always type up the rules and put them through a poster maker at Kinko's or some other printing service. It's a tax write-off!

The following lists contain a few general teacher guidelines and student rules for using wall charts.

Working the Walls

1. At first you will need to remind students of the wall-chart rules.
2. You must move your body to the spot where the wall chart hangs.
3. Students should watch you write on the wall chart.
4. If you marked a chart in a previous class, it is important that you point to it and explain how you added to it today.
5. It's best to have a specific reason to introduce or to add to a wall chart.
6. Students should add to wall charts to keep them growing.
7. Revisit the rules often. When you see an example in readings or in student writing, highlight it. Encourage students to do the same.
8. Over the year, use those odd moments at the end of class or while waiting for the assembly to start to review posted items in the classroom.

Student Rules for Wall Charts and Posters

- Use wall charts and posters while you write.
- Know that if it's on the wall, it's important.
- Know it's not cheating to look at the wall charts; that's why they're there.
- Attempt to make the walls a part of your mind.

Integrating Wall Charts into Teaching Throughout the Year

Wall charts and posters should go up not all at once, but one at a time over the first months of school and anytime you find a new need. These posters and wall charts should be revisited often while reading, while correcting sentences, while drafting, while editing. I continually highlight them by pointing at them, tapping on them, having students chorally read them, asking what effect the writer's choices have. My job is to make using these mechanics like breathing for students: Exposure is the key.

My classroom walls are a gigantic scaffold, a place to hang and categorize new knowledge, to see connections, to form patterns. From *Sentence Patterns* to *Capitalization Rules* to a high-frequency word wall, my wall charts and posters help ensure that students have the scaffolding they need to become adept users of the English language. This multidimensional, visual strategy, anchored in brain-based learning, has revolutionized my grammar and mechanics teaching. Grounding students in visual print, marinating them in the context of examples, and highlighting what is important in the multitude of grammar and mechanics rules—these strategies have revolutionized my students' learning as well.

Constructing Lessons: Background, Mentor Text, and Visual Scaffolds

The lessons that follow serve as a scaffold. Maybe you need a way into a grammar or mechanics lesson, a mentor text to illustrate a point, a visual to support students' understanding, or maybe you just want to think about the types of errors your students are making and why. Part II is set up to provide you with several resources for teaching crucial grammar and mechanics. Each section on an error or concept contains an operator's manual, mentor text, lesson, and a visual scaffold.

Operator's Manual: The operator's manual is designed for the teacher, the driver of instruction. It provides background on the error or concept, as well as pertinent information that a teacher may need when navigating the teaching of the error or concept. Each operator's manual contains four types of information:

- *In Plain English:* I define the error or concept in language that is as plain as possible.
- *AKA or Also Known As:* I give other names that often refer to the error or concept.
- *Student Error:* I include an example of a student error to show common mistakes student writers make.
- *Behind the Error:* I look beyond the actual error and consider what might be causing the student to make the error. I share pseudo-concepts and common missing links that block understanding of this error or concept.

After linking the concept to typical student errors, I present instructional ideas and resources for teaching about the error or concept.

Mentor Text: Mentor text shows the error in another light: the light of correctness. If students are going to stare at writing and talk about it, they must see powerful writing models. In this section, I provide such models, using boldface type to highlight the textual elements that relate to the error or concept under discussion.

Lessons: The lessons give starting points—marking texts, imitation, and alternate ways of looking at the concept by using strong mentor texts. While it is ideal for lessons to emerge out of student writing, I know that I often needed suggestions from other teachers to get me started. These are some lessons that have helped my kids (and me) on our journey toward correctness. They allow for experimentation beyond simple sentences and provide scaffolds to help writers find their voices.

Visual Scaffold: Every lesson is followed by a visual scaffold. This cue supports the lesson by using visual patterns to help enhance students' abilities to make connections, see patterns, and repeat those patterns in their own writing. Some of the scaffolds might become the starting points for wall charts; others are designed to be cut and pasted into student writer's notebooks.

The following lessons are a menu to pick and choose from. Many of these processes and methods work for other writing issues. You may use the lessons with the whole class, small groups, or individuals.

The Sentence:
A Way of Thinking

In biblical times, the word sentence *was defined as "a way of thinking."*

Oxford English Dictionary

Consider the sentence a story, a mini-yarn, with a beginning and ending and a dramatic arc.

Writing affords us a luxury we lack in conversation: we can go back and recast our sentences, paying attention to syntax and sensuality in a way that's impossible when you are expounding extemporaneously.

Constance Hale, Sin and Syntax

You don't need an encyclopedic knowledge of grammatical terms to write and edit with precision. I couldn't diagram a sentence if my life depended on it.

Bill Walsh, Lapsing into a Comma

A sentence should be alive. . . . Sentences need energy to make the meaning jump off the page and into the reader's head. As a writer you must embed energy in the sentence—coil the spring, set the trap.

Peter Elbow, Writing with Power

63

1.1 Fragments

In Plain English   A sentence must contain at least one subject and one verb, and it must form a complete thought. A fragment is missing a subject or verb, and/or it doesn't contain a complete thought.

AKA   Incomplete sentence, non-sentence, intentional fragment.

Writers should master the complete-sentence technique before getting fragment-happy.
—Bill Walsh, *The Elephants of Style*

A fragment is not a sentence. It may have a capital letter. It may even have a period, but it's missing an important element, such as a subject or a verb. Fragments may add rhythm, emphasis, and variety to writing—when they're intentional—and some-times even when they're not. However, students need the ability to fix sentence frag-ments. They must be able to identify them and avoid writing them in high-stakes situ-ations such as testing. Sentence fragments may also make writing appear sloppy and incorrect. Students need to distinguish between the effective use of fragments, which is purposeful and rare, and the ineffective use, which looks careless and choppy.

To identify and correct fragments, writers must understand the simple sentence. They don't need to mark all the parts of speech or make a diagram. Students do need to know that a group of words starting with a capital letter and ending with a period is not necessarily a complete sentence. When I ask students what makes a sentence a sentence, they respond: "Letters," "A capital at the beginning," and "Periods." But what do they really know about the sentence?

Do they know that a minimal simple sentence must have a subject and a verb? *Sean laughs.* That's a simple sentence. We could add a few prepositional phrases such as *at* The Real World *blaring **from** his plasma screen TV*. While those preposi-tional phrases add detail, they are not needed to form a simple sentence. Everything students learn about sentences, from compound to complex, rides on this essential understanding: Simple sentences are made up of a subject and verb. *Sean laughs.* Who or what laughs? Sean, the subject. What does he do? Laughs, the verb.

The ability to pare a sentence down to its essential core is the first tool students need in order to uncover the craft of all sentences.

Student Error   *When I was five. I had a Chuckie doll. I would scare everybody with Chuckie. Chuckie was about two feet, had orange hair, little red and white shoes, overalls, and plastic knife. I replaced the plastic knife with a real knife. To make Chuckie look more like the real thing. From the kitchen Drawer. Like a mini-butcher knife. I super glued it into Chuckie's hand. Ready for business.*

Behind the Error   This is a typical student attempt at adding sophistication to sentences. Randy doesn't want to use only simple sentences. He wants to add some life and complexity to his sentences, but in taking this risk, he creates fragments with his punctuation. Have you ever wondered why kids in fourth grade start writing fragments? Their skills aren't keeping up with their growing intellect and their ability to express ever-more-complex thoughts. Randy writes: *When I was five. I had a Chuckie doll.* We should celebrate that he's stumbled on the complex sentence. His thinking needs this more sophisticated sentence form. On the surface, we see a fragment, and if we were bean counting, we might see that he's writing more fragments now than he did a year ago, but a lot of these fragments are fragments because Randy is punctuating the dependent clause with a period instead of a comma. When students hit this stage, they are ready for more tools to express themselves.

Mentor Text   *They race.* (p. 5)
—Jerry Spinelli, *Loser*

Matt winces. (p. 364)
Maria flinched. (p. 366)
Matt froze. (p. 370)
Matt nodded. (p. 372)
—Nancy Farmer, *House of the Scorpion*

Tad watched. (p. 6)
Blood flew. (p. 111)
He sprung. (p. 128)
—Stephen King, *Cujo*

LESSON

Two-Word Sentence Smack Down

I ask students to write a sentence in their writer's notebooks—just one sentence. After a minute, I ask, "What'd you do?" After they share, I ask, "How did you know that was a sentence? What makes a sentence a sentence?" We discuss the fact that most of us know how to write a sentence, even if we can't explain why. I emphasize that the point of grammar is to help us write. Though we need not know every single definition, we should know a few. Competent, confident writers know that an underlying structure holds some thoughts together and separates others. So, students need to be able to break down a sentence. This knowledge is the foundation for taking writing from choppy to flowing, from run-on to controlled. Understanding this pattern is essential, for every craft move is built on it.

"You know sentences. Everyone wrote a sentence. Even those who said, *I don't know what to write* were saying a sentence. It's basic to our human nature to speak in sentences."

"So, why is it so difficult to figure them out on tests?" I ask. We discuss an over-simplified formula for the sentence: *subject + verb = a simple sentence.* It's easy to lose students' attention when we talk in abstractions, so I get their eyes on a sentence from a book as soon as possible. Using a sentence from Spinelli's *Loser,* I explain the sentence test, which will allow us to strip any sentence down to its core, subject and verb. I write *They race* on the board. "Is that a sentence? How do you know?" I explain that it's a sentence if it provides answers to the following two questions:

- Who or what did or is something? (The subject is *They.*)
- What did they do or what are they? (The verb is *race.*)

"The core of any sentence is a subject and a verb," I say. I preselect a few longer sentences from *Loser* that students can shave down to two words: a subject and a verb. We pare down a few together first, such as this one: *The lights cluster brilliantly up the street at Claudia's house* (p. 174). Using the test, we determine that the subject is *lights* and the verb is *cluster*.

"Now we're ready to do a sentence smack down!" I say. Before class, I have made a wall mat like the one in the visual scaffold, with the categories "subject" and "verb." To make this activity more exciting, I play some snippets of music from a sports mix. The music adds a feeling of joy to the room, taking the dread out of grammar instruction. I play the music and yell, "Are you ready to grammar?" The music continues to play while students work with their sentences and during each transition. I put a kid in charge of the music, so I am free to emcee.

First, I divide students into groups of three and give each group a sentence (see the Appendix for the "Sentence Smack Down!" handout). Each group then follows the handout directions. After paring down their sentence, they use construction paper to record the subject on one sheet and the verb on the other. After the kids finish with the construction paper, I explain that one member of each group must assume the role of the reader, and the other two will play the parts of "subject" and "verb." Then I describe how each performance will go:

- The reader will read the whole sentence.
- The "subject" will "smack," or slap, the wall mat under the word "subject" and yell the subject of the group's sentence.
- The "verb" will follow, "smacking" the wall mat under the word "verb" and yelling the verb of the sentence.
- The reader will read the whole sentence again.

To illustrate, a group takes a sentence: *He reaches back to touch the door.* The group pares the sentence down to the subject (*He*) and verb (*reaches*). After choosing roles, the "subject" writes *He* large enough for the class to see on one piece of construction paper. The "verb" writes *reaches* and surrounds it with exploding marks to connote action.

When called to the front, the reader reads, "He reaches back to touch the door." Next, the "subject" runs and smacks the subject side of the wall mat, yelling out "he" as well as holding up the piece of construction paper. After that, the "verb" smacks the verb side of the wall mat, yelling out "reaches." These two hold their positions at the wall mat, while the reader reads the entire sentence again.

Two-Word Sentence Search—Powerful Words, Powerful Verbs

As a follow-up, I challenge students to collect two-word sentences from their reading; this will become a yearlong collection. We post the collection on a wall chart—it's the skinniest wall chart ever. It is fun to watch students find out how rare two-word sentences are and to witness everything else they discover along the way. When students bring what they think is a two-word sentence to me, such as *Or not,* I ask the sentence-test questions: Who or what did something? What did they do? Students have no answer. "Is it a sentence then?" A light goes on in their eyes, and they know it's a fragment. Of course, we exclude dialogue from this collection, but we do have valuable conversations about dialogue tags as parts of sentences.

My favorite craft spillover is that most two-word sentences have powerful verbs, so we have mentor sentences that we can either expand or allow to remain elegant and simple. Students will finally own the core sentence.

A great mentor text for two-word sentences is the pop-up picture book *Worms Wiggle* by David Pelham and Michael Foreman (1989), which is ripe for imitation if one has the inclination.

Visual Scaffold

Simple Sentence Smack Down
Two students "smack" the subject and verb distilled from their *Loser* sentence. I developed this exercise by combining and modifying lessons from my colleague Alana Morris of Aldine ISD and Mina Shaughnessy (1977).

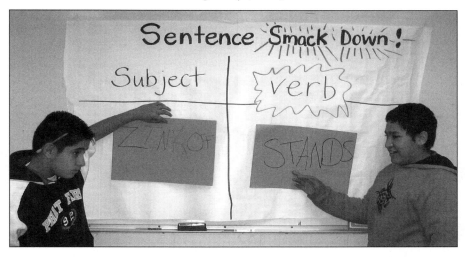

Two-Word Sentence Collection
The students and I keep a collection of two-word sentences we come across in our reading. I return to this wall chart again and again whenever I want to revisit what the "core" of a sentence is.

1.2 Run-On Sentences

OPERATOR'S MANUAL

In Plain English   A run-on sentence is created when two or more independent clauses are placed together without proper punctuation or connectors. Connectors may be transition words or coordinating and subordinating conjunctions.

AKA   Fused sentences, lack of end marks, lack of punctuation, stringy sentences, "and-then-itus" (strings of "and then" in place of periods).

Playing with long sentences does not mean ignoring basic rules.
—Constance Hale, *Sin and Syntax*

Strunk and White (2000) advise "Omit needless words. Vigorous writing is concise" (p. 23). On the other hand, James Moffett (1987) reminds us, "Sentences must grow rank before they can be trimmed" (p. 172). What is a writer to do? Run-on and fused sentences are borne of student excitement and a steady flow of ideas. Students may even write an entire paper as one run-on sentence. I wish there were a trick to fix this problem, such as asking the student to read it aloud and point out where he or she pauses. Often, though, they don't pause. Run-on sentences are both a reading and writing issue. Novice writers and readers don't have a sense of how language ebbs and flows, pauses and stops; however, we must remember to celebrate their flowing thoughts and ideas first.

If you're lucky, students are just being sloppy, leaving out the periods because of carelessness. But more than likely, the problem stems from the students' lack of familiarity with the base sentence. They can't find the independent clause. These students may not have a sense of how to make sentences contain more information, to navigate beyond simple sentences.

When students want to add more information to their sentences but don't have the tools to do so, it's a teachable moment for craft instruction. By studying mentor sentences, students gain the desire to craft flowing sentences, some short, some long. They discover the secrets for adding information to sentences without creating sentences that run on.

Student Error   *Something that makes me happy is my friend Destiny she doesn't try to act all cool and she is just goofy like when she dances she don't care about what nobody says and she just does dirty dancing and laughs and doesn't worry so she is a lot of fun to hang with because she makes me laugh and we can go to Ingram Park mall and cruise around she is not shy so we always get to meet guys.*

Behind the Error   Desiree has a lot to say about her friend Destiny. In fact, Desiree is almost breathless in writing her thoughts down on the page. Most likely, her sentence boundary issues have to do with her lack of understanding of a simple sentence. She needs strategies to put into manageable chunks all the details that flow so easily.

Mentor Text   *They handle the BB gun carelessly,* **trading it back and forth, each slinging the barrel over his shoulder like a hunter in a frontier television show.** (p. 1)

They are shouting your name, **asking if dinner is ready yet.** (p. 1)
—Jim Grimsley, *Winter Birds*

And Furlough found his brother in the library, **standing on top of the great open book, his tail wrapped tightly around his feet, his small body shivering.** (p. 46)
—Kate DiCamillo, *The Tale of Despereaux*

Abraham was growing fast, **shooting up like a sunflower, a spindly youngster with big boney hands, unruly black hair, a dark complexion, and luminous gray eyes.** (p. 11)
—Russell Freedman, *Lincoln: A Photobiography*

She stands there, **staring at the lake, knowing that her dad is gone forever.**
—Justin, sixth grader

LESSON

Dependent Vs. Independent—Adding On Without Running On

We discuss the definition of dependence first, connecting to their lives and whom they depend on to take care of them. "When you get older, you will no longer be dependent. You will stand on your own. That's the whole point of school—to make you independent." A sentence has to earn its independence by having a subject and a verb and a complete thought. Sentences are independent, and fragments are dependent—they can't stand on their own.

I write a sentence from *Winter Birds* on the overhead: *They handle the BB gun carelessly.* We go through the sentence test and add the question, "Does it express a complete thought?" The students discuss how the sentence stands on its own. Michael says, "It doesn't leave you hangin'."

I write *trading it back and forth* on the overhead. We give it the sentence test and it fails. Priscilla squints, "It leaves you hangin'."

We talk about how these words can't stand on their own but how dependent things *can* lean on independent things. Students realize they are dependent on someone who's independent and that you can attach dependent things to independent things. I attach *trading it back and forth* with a comma: *They handle the BB gun carelessly, trading it back and forth.* We discuss how we can often attach dependent things that can't stand on their own to independent things they can lean on.

To demonstrate the sentence's power, I stop the analyzing, have kids shut their eyes, and ask them to see the sentence as I read it aloud, see the way the structures act like a camera, gliding across a scene, getting a close-up of the details.

> **They handle the BB gun carelessly,** *trading it back and forth, each slinging the barrel over his shoulder like a hunter in a frontier television show.*

Then we look at the sentence again, up close, and I say I will show them how to control the camera as they write. We add pictures to our sentences, and create mind movies by making additions to our sentences without running on. "Notice how the groups of words are both separated by the commas and held together by them," I point out.

Visual Scaffold   **Sentence Closer Graphic**
Students aren't often taught this comma rule, which is the basis for many effective professionally written sentences.

Core Sentence + additions attached and grouped with commas

Independent clause (sentence) + dependents

1.3 Dangling Modifiers

OPERATOR'S MANUAL

In Plain English   Modifiers are words or phrases that describe or modify part of a sentence. Modifiers dangle when it's not clear what they describe. Modifiers usually need to be near the idea (noun) they are meant to describe or modify. Correctly placed modifiers sharpen the images of sentences and combine multiple ideas or actions in one sentence.

AKA   Dangling participles, misplaced modifiers.

Just the words *dangling modifiers* are enough to send chills down most spines. I have a vague memory of a teacher saying, "your modifier is dangling," and of looking down to see if my pants were zipped.

It's simple, really. Modifiers change a sentence's structure and meaning. They should be placed as close as possible to the noun they modify, in order to prevent confusion. Here is an example of a dangling modifier: *Jumping up and down on the bed, the lamp broke.* Unless this is a fantasy story, the lamp isn't jumping up and down. *Jumping up and down on the bed, my brother knocked over the lamp.* To keep the modifier *jumping up and down* from dangling, I add *my brother* because he was the one jumping up and down, not the lamp.

Dangling modifiers cause confusion because the reader doesn't know the writer's intended message. In *Anguished English* (1989), Richard Lederer uses the following example to show how dangling or misplaced modifiers can cause confusion:

> *Yoko Ono will talk about her husband, John Lennon, who was killed in an interview with Barbara Walters.* (p. 150)

The modifier *who was killed* is near *John Lennon* as appropriate, but the modifier *in an interview with Barbara Walters* should be moved to the front of the sentence—unless we mean to communicate that Ms. Walters's interviews are more hard-hitting than we realized.

Student Error   *Barking like a burglar was breaking in, I checked on the dog.*

Behind the Error   Instead of cringing at this error, I remember that there is so much to celebrate. Jorge begins his sentence with a participial phrase, and he indicates a cause-effect relationship in one sentence.

Mentor Text   **Barking furiously,** *Cujo gave chase.* (p. 18)
Cujo trailed at Brett's heels, **looking hot and dispirited.** (p. 46)
Cujo stood at the edge of the lawn, **his great head lowered, his eyes reddish and filmy, growling.** (p. 110)
—Stephen King, *Cujo*

The dog stood up like a lion, **stiff-standing hackles, teeth uncovered as he lashed up his fury for the charge.** (p. 166)
—Zora Neale Hurston, *Their Eyes Were Watching God*

And this particular afternoon, I'm about halfway up the road along the river when I see something out of the corner of my eye. Something moves. I look, and about fifteen *yards off, there's this shorthaired dog—**white with brown and black spots—not making any kind of noise, just slinking along with his head down, watching me, tail between his legs like he's hardly got the right to breathe.** A beagle, maybe a year or two old.*

I stop and the dog stops. Looks like he's been caught doing something awful, when I can tell all he really wants is to follow along beside me.

*"Here, boy," I say, **slapping my thigh.***

*Dog goes down on his stomach, **groveling about in the grass.** I laugh and start over toward him. He's got an old worn-out collar on, **probably older than he is.** Bet it belonged to another dog before him.*

*"C'mon," I say, **putting out my hand.***

*The dog up and backs off. He don't even whimper, **like he's lost his bark.*** (p. 4)
—Phyllis Reynolds Naylor, *Shiloh*

LESSON

Only You Can Prevent Dangling Modifiers— Playing with Sentence Parts

Prior to sharing the mentor text, I want the kids to practice visualizing sentences. "Close your eyes and picture a dog approaching you," I say. Once students have a picture, they open their eyes. On the board I write: *The dog approached me.* "That's an okay sentence. However, we can add action, pictures, or sounds to our sentences or make them like mini-movies. One way to do this is to add *-ing* verbs (Noden 1999) to our sentences." Writing "*-ing* verbs" on the board, I ask, "What are some *-ing* verbs that describe what a dog does?" We list them on board (see visual scaffold).

I have students close their eyes again, and I say: "Barking, growling, snarling, the dog approached me." I repeat it a couple of times. Once students open their eyes, I ask whether the picture in their minds changed. "Why do you think it changed?" Students share that the *-ing* verbs added action, movement, pictures, or sounds. Next we move the *-ing* verbs to the end of the sentence and discuss which we like better. Then, we play around with an *-ing* clause, *wagging its tail,* moving it from the end to the beginning and then a new place, the middle.

After that, I share the mentor sentences and let students move the phrases and clauses (the dependent chunks of the sentence) around and see the effects of the different placements.

As a follow-up, we look at sentences from *Cujo* and *Shiloh,* noting the differences in tone and modifier placement, continuing the metaphor of the camera zooming in, focusing on the sentence and not the labels.

Visual Scaffold

The Dog Approached Me with *–ing* Verbs
After I write the sentence *The dog approached me* on the board, students brainstorm all the *-ing* verbs that a dog can do.

The dog approached me.

-ing verbs

barking	wagging its tail
growling	slobbering
snarling	panting
scratching at the ground	jumping

Location, Location, Location!
Students move sentence parts around to see the possible placement patterns, discovering the differing effects and punctuation.

Opener	Interrupter	Closer
Wagging its tail, **the dog approached me.**	**The dog,** wagging its tail, **approached me.**	**The dog approached me,** wagging its tail.

1.4 Wrong or Missing Preposition

OPERATOR'S MANUAL

In Plain English   A preposition shows the relationship between a noun and other words in a sentence. Some teachers say a preposition is everywhere a cat can go: *above, around, behind, beneath, in, toward, outside, over, under,* and *with.* Prepositions make our writing clearer, orienting the reader in time and space, showing relationships. Prepositions may serve as transitions between ideas as well. Leaving out a preposition or using the wrong one makes readers stumble.

AKA   Incorrect prepositions, prepositions where they don't belong (*should of* instead of the correct contraction—*should've*).

Prepositional phrases in prose can be grounding, but they can also make passages soar—especially when they are used discriminately and groomed carefully.
—Constance Hale, *Sin and Syntax*

If students continue having trouble with run-on sentences or identifying the subject and the verb in a sentence, presenting students with information about prepositional phrases may help. In the context of phrases, students will be more exposed to and attentive to which prepositions work with which phrases. Prepositional phrases certainly expand sentences. In fact, Texas's state writing standards suggest that students learn to elaborate sentences with prepositional phrases. Whether we want to elaborate or to simplify sentences, a working knowledge of prepositional phrases is essential.

To help students see the work that prepositions do in sentences, I make a fun paragraph such as the one below.

> My neighbor said she wanted to ask me **for** a small favor. Little did I know what was **in** store **for** me when I agreed to feed her cat. **After** my neighbor left **on** her trip, I walked **across** the street **to** her house. Once I got **inside** the house, I was overwhelmed **by** the stench **of** cat urine. I looked **around** the house and couldn't believe what I saw. My eyes fell **on** two salad dressing containers sitting **on** a table **beside** the couch, which was completely covered **with** dirty laundry, **except for** this one worn area **by** the table. The volume **on** the TV was turned up all the way. **In** disbelief and **despite** my better judgment, I walked **toward** the restroom. **Around** the base **of** the tub, I saw these red velvety mushrooms coming up **between** the tub and tile floor. This filth was **beyond** anything I'd ever seen **in** my life. **Within** two minutes, the cat was fed and I was out **of** there. Since she returned **from** her trip, I have never been available to watch her cat again.

For more on prepositions, see the "List of Common Prepositions" in the visual scaffold. A reproducible version is included in the Appendix.

Student Error   *We were going towards San Antonio, but we stopped at San Marcos to eat the McDonald's.*

Behind the Error   Spanish uses only one preposition, *en,* in all sentences, which might confuse things for Vincent, a native of Mexico. He does know that prepositions show relationships between words. He knows that both *at* and *in* show place, but he needs some help with using *in* with a city, not *at*. For the most part, students learn more about prepositions in the context of using them to add detail to their sentences and proofing their writing for missing ones.

Mentor Text   **Big Hair Style 3: The Texan**
Take the teasing comb and back-comb all your hair until it looks like an electrified Persian cat. To tease your hair, grab a small section and hold it up by the end. Comb downward with the teasing comb in short fast strokes until it gets tangled at the bottom. Pull the teased hair up and out to achieve maximum altitude. Liberally apply the hair spray to hold the teased hair in place. If you can still see the walls, you haven't sprayed enough. Spray more. All these styles must be taken care of while you sleep. Some women use the beehive hairnet; others use feather pillows to sleep upon; while still others sleep upright in the La-Z-Boy. Your mileage may vary. Just be careful not to put anyone's eye out. (pp. 4–5)
—Kinky Friedman, *Kinky Friedman's Guide to Texas Etiquette*

Big Hair Style 3: The Texan Without Prepositional Phrases
Take the teasing comb and back-comb all your hair. To tease your hair, grab a small section and hold it. Comb downward. Pull the teased hair. Liberally apply the hair spray. If you can still see the walls, you haven't sprayed enough. Spray more. All these styles must be taken care of while you sleep. Some women use the beehive hairnet; others use feather pillows; while still others sleep upright. Your mileage may vary. Just be careful not to put anyone's eye out.

LESSON

I've Got a Preposition for You

To begin the lesson, I ask, "How important are prepositions?" If I get blank stares, I know we have to do some defining and I will use something familiar to students, such as "all the places a cat can go," or "all the places an eighth grader can go between classes."

The first thing I do is share a piece of text with and without prepositional phrases so that students can see their impact. The Kinky Friedman piece drops almost 30 percent in size without prepositional phrases—from 130 words to 83. Students notice that we lose the visuals when we take out the prepositions, which is the perfect time to discuss how prepositions and their phrases orient us in time and space. After handing out the list of common prepositions (see the visual scaffold), I ask whether any students think they can describe a room, a painting, or a process without prepositions. If someone won't try, I will. And I ask students to "catch" me when I say a preposition.

Next, depending on students' confidence, I may share the story describing my neighbor's house (the one given in the Operator's Manual). Students follow this by writing their own descriptions, using as many prepositional phrases as possible. If I feel that students are still writing run-ons because they don't understand the basics of a sentence, I have them take a piece of text, and, with a partner, put parentheses around each prepositional phrase so that it is easier to identify the main subject and verb of sentences.

Visual Scaffold

List of Common Prepositions

Categorized lists help students get to know prepositions and understand their functions.

	Location		Time	Other Relationships
above	beyond	outside	after	about
across	by	over	as	despite
against	down	past	before	except
along	from	through	during	for
among	in	to	since	like
around	inside	toward	until	of
at	into	under		per
behind	near	underneath		than
below	off	up		with
beside	on	within		without
between	out			

1.5 Double Negative

OPERATOR'S MANUAL

In Plain English A double negative occurs when two negative words are used incorrectly in a sentence.

AKA Multiple negations.

Two negative words tend to cancel each other and create a positive meaning, which may not be what you have in mind.
—Jan Venolia, *Write Right*

He *didn't* tell *nobody*. *Didn't* and *nobody* are both negative words. To correct the error, we take out one negative word, either one, and the sentence becomes *He didn't tell anyone* or *He told no one.*

Patricia O'Conner (1996) points out that we should never say never on double negatives. (I just used two *nevers.*) We don't say: *I don't have no grades for this week.* But have you ever said something along the lines of *I wouldn't say he was uncooperative?* Then, you've used a double negative, but that double negative serves to soften the message. Personally, I'd never tell my students that the double negative is sometimes useful. I just want them to stop saying, "I don't got no paper." No need to dwell on the fact that Shakespeare and Chaucer used the double negative, though we may explain that Robert Lowth, a professor at Oxford University who has greatly influenced grammar instruction from the 1700s until today, simply decided we couldn't have double negatives for reasons of logic—two negatives equal a positive.

From a craft perspective, leaving a double negative in dialogue can be an excellent choice. It can reveal much about a character. But in formal writing and speaking, the double negative should be avoided.

Student Error *She didn't have no lunch, and I felt sorry for her.*

Behind the Error The student is following a pattern of grammar that has its own rules, not Standard English rules, but rules just the same. Some languages, such as French and Spanish, use the double negative. This is an opportunity to teach students about the formal and informal registers of language, and how they are handled differently in other languages, without disrespecting student dialect.

Mentor Text *"I got plenty of chores need doing around here this morning," his mother announced as they were finishing the grits and red gravy. His mother was from Georgia and still cooked like it.*

"Oh, Momma!" Ellie and Brenda squawked in concert. Those girls could get out of work faster than a grasshopper could slip through your fingers.

"Momma, you promised me and Brenda we could go to Millsburg for school shopping."

"You ain't got no money for school shopping!"

"Momma. We're just going to look around." Lord, he wished Brenda would stop whining so. "Christmas! You don't want us to have no fun at all."

"Any fun," Ellie corrected her primly.

"Oh, shuttup."

Ellie ignored her. "Miz Timmons is coming to pick us up. I told Lollie Sunday you said it was OK. I feel dumb calling her and saying you changed your mind."

"Oh, all right. But I ain't got no money to give you."

Any money, something whispered in Jess's head. "I know, Momma. We'll just take the five dollars Daddy promised us. No more'n that." (pp. 6–7)
—Katherine Paterson, *Bridge to Terabithia*

Register Swap—The Formal and Informal Registers

"What can Katherine Paterson teach us with this passage?" I ask. We discuss how she can teach us about dialogue rules, real-sounding dialogue, using other words instead of *said,* and the double negative. "What's going on with the correcting?" I ask. "Why do you think Jess and Ellie correct the sister, Brenda, and not the mother, at least out loud?"

We discuss the difference between formal and informal registers of language: We talk with our friends or with our family one way, which may be different from how we're expected to talk in school. "Do you know what *formal* means?" We discuss the meanings and list some times when it's okay to be informal and some occasions when it is important to be formal. I ask, "If I were in a job interview, what might an employer think about me if I used the double negative?"

Directing students to a closer reading of the passage, I ask them to tell me all the double negatives they see. I use a wall chart, with *informal* written on one side and *formal* on the other, to capture their answers. I copy the double negatives from the excerpt on the informal side. "How could we change these sentences to the formal register?" I ask. Students suggest revisions to sentences, and I write each of these on the formal side, to the right of its informal equivalent.

"On the other hand, don't the double negatives that Momma and Brenda use reveal something about the characters?" We discuss the use of double negative in dialogue and its effectiveness in communicating information about a character in a *showing* rather than *telling* way.

At the end of the lesson, I say, "Let's add this to our editor's checklist: *Avoid the double negative.*"

Visual Scaffold   **Negative Word List**

Often students don't notice a double negative because they don't know that words such as *barely* and *never* are negative words. The list helps them see this problem and correct it, if it is a problem in their writing.

Sneaky Negative Words		
barely	none	Contractions that end in *n't* are also negative words.
hardly	nor	
neither	not	
never	nothing	wouldn't
nobody	nowhere	didn't
		can't
		won't

1.6 The Absolute

In Plain English   An absolute is a free modifier that is grammatically independent of the sentence and is set off by a comma(s). In the simplest terms, an absolute is a noun + an *-ing* verb (Noden 1999).

AKA   Absolute construction or free modifier.

"Absolute" from Latin absolvere, *denoting loose or free from.*
—Theodore Bernstein, *The Careful Writer*

Brilliantly simplified and defined by Noden (1999) as a noun + an *-ing* verb, the absolute adds a close-up camera shot to your sentence. The comma acts as a zoom lens, focusing the reader's visualization on something small in the larger wide-angle shot of the sentence, as in the one that follows: **Leg going up and down, pencil tapping against the metal,** *Garrett waits for silent sustained reading to be over.*

Christensen (1968) describes other ways to create an absolute. Lest you think that a noun + an *-ing* or *-ed* verb is the only form of an absolute, here are all the variations Christensen found in popular and classic literature:

- Noun + an *-ing, -ed,* or *-en* verb (*lip quivering, fist knotted, heart broken*)
- Noun + an adverb (*head down, hat off*)
- Noun + an adjective (*head sweaty, shirt white and crisp*)
- Noun + a preposition (*pen in hand*)
- Preposition (usually *with* or *like*) + noun + any of the above variations (*with hair standing up on the back of her neck*)
- Possessive pronoun + noun + any of the above variations (*his knees drawn to his chest*)

In each construction, the comma that must set off the absolute acts like a camera's zoom lens, focusing on some small detail that enriches the image the writer is attempting to produce in the reader's mind.

Student Error   *Mind working anxiety rising I took my math benchmark for what seemed like the millionth time this year.*

Behind the Error   Miguel has mastered the absolute construction: He uses it as an opener and it makes a more complex sentence. By asking him to read it, I can help him discover that he is pausing, and we can talk about how to show the reader a pause with a comma.

Mentor Text   **Birds still sang, flowers still bloomed, cows still slept** *in the meadow, and I ate soup—now cold—as if my mama hadn't ever gone.* (p. 13)
—Patricia MacLachlan, *Journey*

"And on my honor," Bear said, **his voice booming, his arms spread wide.** (p. 172)
—Avi, *Crispin*

LESSON

The Absolute Zoom Lens—A Think- and Look-Aloud

I start the teaching of the absolute with images: pictures of family or from magazines. Noden's (1999) argument that the absolute is a zoom lens guides my teaching of it. I start with a picture of my favorite hobby. For me, bike riding is the only thing that ever stills my mind.

As the students look at the image, I say, "If I were going to make a simple sentence out of this, I would write *The bicyclist raced*. Maybe I'd even add *down the road* at the end of the sentence: *The bicyclist raced down the road*."

I go on with my think-aloud. "That's an okay sentence, but I have learned that the more concrete, specific nouns I have in my writing, the more likely I am to communicate the picture I have in my head and create pictures in my readers' heads." I explain that in my reading I have noticed something writers seem to always do, but there is nothing in our English book to tell me about it. "What writers do is find a smaller noun that's in the wide-angle shot of the sentence, and then they add an *-ing* verb to that noun."

"Ya'll are quick learners, so let's just do it," I say. We look at the picture again and see that there are lots of "little" nouns in our wide-angle shot. We list them on the board: *legs, pedals, wheels, street, sweat, face, hands*. I leave a space next to each item on the board. "Now, let's add an *-ing* verb to each noun," I say, and we come up with: *legs pumping, pedals spinning, wheels turning, street making a ribbon into the horizon, sweat dripping, face grimacing, hands gripping the handlebars*. Students naturally start adding little phrases.

We evaluate the noun and *-ing* pairs and pick two to attach to a sentence. We try them in the opener and closer positions:

Legs pumping, sweat dripping, the bicyclist raced down the road.

The bicyclist raced down the road, **legs pumping, sweat dripping.**

Then I hand out pictures I have laminated. First, kids write the wide-angle shot simple sentence. After that, they go back and find the "little" nouns that are part of the big picture—literally—and make a list. Next, students add *-ing* verbs or phrases to their "little" nouns, and then they pick their favorite combinations and connect one or two to a sentence. We start with the opener or closer positions, and add interrupting positions when it seems appropriate, connecting back to the sentence pattern charts.

I require that students try an absolute in their next writing assignment and that they highlight it when submitting it for assessment. But, for the most part, they would do it without the requirement because they love how sophisticated their writing sounds with that little grammatical addition, which they see as a close-up camera shot.

Visual Scaffold   **Brainstorm of Nouns and *–ing* Verbs**

After brainstorming the nouns, students brainstorm *-ing* verbs that go with each noun. Then they select the best two combinations to add to the sentence.

Nouns We See	*-ing* Verbs Related to These Nouns
Pedals	spinning, pumping, turning
Hands	gripping, gripping handlebars
Wheels (spokes)	spinning, splashing, turning, skidding
Face	grunting, dripping with sweat, covered in mud*
Legs	pumping, standing, grinding
Sweat	dripping, staining, soaking his shirt
Mud	splattering, flying, dripping, covering his legs

*A student will always quite accidentally discover that participles (what we've called *-ing* verbs) also have a past form (*-ed* and *-en*).

Pause and Effect:
Crafting Sentences with Commas

There is nothing much to punctuating a sentence, really, beyond a little comma sense. Get the commas right, and the rest will fall into place.

Patricia O'Conner, *Woe Is I*

There are hard-and-fast rules about commas, of course, but within those rules there is plenty of room for nuance and interpretation.

Bill Walsh, *Lapsing into a Comma*

The rule is: don't use commas like a stupid person. I mean it. More than any other mark, the comma requires the writer to use intelligent discretion and to be simply alert to potential ambiguity.

Lynne Truss, *Eats, Shoots & Leaves*

A misplaced comma can create more confusion than a conversation with a teenager.
Laurie E. Rozakis, *The Complete Idiot's Guide to Grammar and Style*

2.1 No Comma in a Compound Sentence

OPERATOR'S MANUAL

In Plain English   Use a comma and a coordinating conjunction to join two independent clauses. Conjunctions are connectors that link equal words, phrases, or clauses. Coordinating conjunctions cue readers in on the relationships between ideas.

AKA   Run-on sentence.

Commas are used when two complete sentences are joined together, using such conjunctions as and, or, but, while, *or* yet.
—Lynne Truss, *Eats, Shoots & Leaves*

As writers mature, they need more sophisticated ways to express their developing thinking. Enter the compound sentence. Compound sentences show links or connections between two ideas. Students use oral compound sentences correctly long before they can punctuate them. Jennifer will say, "You said grammar would be fun, but this comma stuff is hard." However, when writing the compound sentence, she may not insert the comma after *fun,* making the error of no comma in a compound sentence. The coordinating conjunction is there, but the comma has gone missing.

Editor Bill Walsh (2000) puts it this way, "How do you know when to use a comma when these conjunctions (*and* and *but*) link two clauses? If there's a new subject—or the old subject is restated—use the comma. If the second clause shares a subject with the first (and that subject is not restated), don't use a comma" (pp. 75–76). For example, this sentence from Wendelin Van Draanen's book *Flipped* (2001) is punctuated correctly: *I was relieved, but I also felt like a weenie.* Both sides of the compound sentence have subjects and verbs, and the sentence is joined with a coordinating conjunction, so the sentence needs a comma. On the other hand, if the sentence read *I was relieved but also felt like a weenie,* a comma wouldn't be needed because the subject is not restated in the second half of the sentence nor is a new one added.

Compound sentences are an essential tool in a writer's toolbox. To make this concept easier for my students, I use the mnemonic "FANBOYS" to refer to the coordinating conjunctions: *For, And, Nor, But, Or, Yet, So.* It's easier for my students to remember the mnemonic first, and then connect the FANBOYS to coordinating conjunctions later.

Often students become confused about the use of coordinating conjunctions. Many overgeneralize the rule of using the FANBOYS and a comma to join two independent clauses, believing it to mean that they should place a comma before the FANBOYS any time they are used. They create monstrosities such as: *Crystal, and I walked to Lackland City Trailer Park, and bought Cokes at the Diamond Shamrock.* I lead them back to the visual scaffold again and again, reminding them to use a comma and one of the FANBOYS to join two sentences or independent clauses. (See Section 1.1, Fragments, for more on how to identify a sentence or independent clause.) Another mistake students often make is confusing the meaning of each of the FANBOYS. Each coordinating conjunction has a meaning and shows a specific type of relationship.

Student Error   *I hated the way the water tasted like sand and salt so I didn't let another drop get in my mouth.*

Behind the Error   In writing about her trip to the coast, Ashley senses a link between the idea of not liking how the water tasted and not letting another drop in her mouth. By using *so* as her coordinating conjunction, she also demonstrates her knowledge that *so* shows a cause-effect relationship between the ideas. She knows she doesn't want a period, but she hasn't quite mastered using the comma as well as the coordinating conjunction to link the two ideas. When Ashley inserts the comma after *salt*, her compound sentence won't be missing a thing.

Mentor Text   *Every day was a happy day, **and** every night was peaceful.* (p. 11)
—E. B. White, *Charlotte's Web*

*Celia says you're in shock, **but** I think you're just lazy.* (p. 59)
—Nancy Farmer, *The House of the Scorpion*

*You can pick your friends, **but** you're stuck with family.* (p. 1)
—Jeff Foxworthy, *You Might Be a Redneck If . . . This Is the Biggest Book You've Ever Read*

*Hiccup leapt out of the way, **but** the sharp point of the blade pierced his shirt and tore a neat slice out of it.* (p. 19)
—Cressida Cowell, *How to Be a Pirate*

LESSON

Flipping for the Compound Sentence Pattern

When introducing the compound sentence, I review the simple sentence or independent clause. I use every opportunity to connect the compound sentence to everything they know, from the need for a subject and verb in a sentence to the fact that they use compound sentences every day in their spoken speech: "Mr. Anderson, I got my report card signed, but I didn't bring it."

After reviewing the simple sentence, I ask, "Does anyone know how to make a compound sentence?" After showing them all the ways they know compound sentences, we create a compound sentence wall chart, with graphics and FANBOYS. Then I show students two sentences from *Flipped*:

> *I am still trying to break free, but the girl's got me in a death grip.* (p. 3)
> —Bryce's point of view

> *I chased Bryce up the walkway, and that's when everything changed.* (p. 13)
> —Julianna's perspective

We discuss what students notice about the sentences, pointing out the subjects and verbs on each side of each sentence as well as the commas and coordinating conjunctions. We then compare the sentences to the compound sentence wall chart, and we discuss how each of these sentences needs a comma to complete the whole compound sentence mystique. We take some time to chant the FANBOYS: *for, and, nor, but, or, yet, so.* (My students always appreciate an opportunity for sanctioned loudness.)

Then I write a new pair of sentences on the overhead: *Mr. Anderson, I got my report card signed. I didn't bring it.* I explain that, when we have two ideas that are connected, as writers we may want to join them. "First, as a speaker how would you join the ideas? As a writer? Right, the revision would be: *Mr. Anderson, I got my report card signed, but I didn't bring it.* Why didn't we use *and* or *so*?" Slowly, I start referring to the FANBOYS' meanings as we continue to practice writing compound sentences.

I put up the *Flipped* sentences again without the commas and have students mark where they belong, referring to the wall chart for the language and visual cues to discuss and conceptualize the pattern. After students practice writing a few sentences, they quickly reread a past journal entry or essay and correct any compound sentences that need correcting or find two sentences to combine. We build in the routine of adding every new concept to our living and growing editor's checklist: *Check sentences.*

Later, I take an overly punctuated compound sentence, such as the one shown in AKA of the Operator's Manual, and use it to clarify that using a comma every time we use one of the FANBOYS is an overgeneralization of the rule.

Visual Scaffold

Coordinating Conjunctions Defined Chart

Use a comma and a **conjunction** to join two sentences. The coordinating conjunctions most often used are in boldface type.

Coordinating Conjunctions (FANBOYS)	Relationship Expressed
for, **so**	Shows a cause-effect relationship.
and	Joins things or ideas that are alike or similar, implies a continuation of thought.
but, yet	Shows a contrasting relationship.
or	Indicates a choice between things or ideas.
nor	Continues a negative thought.

Compound Sentence Graphic

Graphic representations make sentence patterns concrete to students by helping them "see" the patterns. This chart was inspired by Joyce Armstrong Carroll and Edward E. Wilson in *Acts of Teaching* (1993). A reproducible "Compound and Serial Comma Sentence Pattern Scaffolds" is provided in the Appendix.

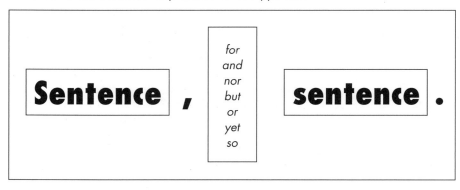

2.2 Comma Splice

OPERATOR'S MANUAL

In Plain English Coordinating conjunctions, such as *and, but,* and *or,* join words and phrases and clauses of equal importance. Even though the comma splice appears to be a repeat of having no comma in a compound sentence, it's not. It's the same song, second verse. This time the error lies in leaving out the coordinating conjunction and using a comma when a semicolon or a period would be more appropriate. In a comma splice, the comma is there, but the conjunction is nowhere to be found.

AKA Comma fault, intentional comma splice.

Equal in grammatical horror to the sentence fragment is the comma splice. A comma splice results when a comma is placed between two independent clauses without the necessary link of a coordinating conjunction.
—Karen Elizabeth Gordon, *The Deluxe Intransitive Vampire*

Once students have learned to use the FANBOYS (*for, and, nor, but, or, yet, so*) to join sentences, they may still leave out the comma—especially after I tell them that we don't use a comma with all of the FANBOYS. There is always an over-do-it backlash anytime I introduce a rule or clarify one.

There also exists an intentional comma splice. Professional authors often use comma splices for rhetorical effect. But in my reality, I know that my students will be tested on a state test that requires them to know the "rule." Personally, I only address the intentional comma splice if a student finds one in a novel and asks about it. If they really want to drop the FANBOYS, they can use a semicolon to join two sentences, as in this example from Livia Bitton-Jackson's *I Have Lived a Thousand Years: Growing Up in the Holocaust* (1999):

> *I no longer attempt to speak to him; I have resigned myself to his silence.*
> (p. 173)

A comma splice can easily be corrected by inserting a semicolon where the comma previously spliced the sentence. Change *I love dancing, it makes me warm inside* (comma splice) to *I love dancing; it makes me warm inside.* The compound sentence pattern helps writers link and combine choppy sentences. It gives a writer the option of joining two sentences with less separation than a period would provide. The two sentences should be linked in some way, and the writer must use a semicolon or a comma and a coordinating conjunction to join them. In the example that follows, notice how the conjunction *but* clues the reader to the link between the two sentences as well as the contrast.

Comma splice: *Felicia balled up the napkin in her fist, she didn't say anything.*

Compound sentence with a comma and a conjunction: *Felicia balled up her napkin in her fist,* **but** *she didn't say anything.*

Compound sentence joined with a semicolon: *Felicia balled up the napkin in her fist; she didn't say anything.*

Student Error

I didn't like the salty water, it was fun swimming in the waves.

Behind the Error

Ashley knows the two ideas are linked, and she wants to show that. She also should be credited for trying to extend her sentences beyond simple choppy ones. She can add one of the FANBOYS after the comma. In this case, her only choice is *but,* which will correctly show the contrast between the two thoughts.

Mentor Text

He could be courteous and helpful on the surface, **but** *you never knew what was going on underneath.* (p. 96)

His voice wasn't loud, **but** *it commanded instant attention.* (p. 99)

Maria had insulted *him in front of everyone,* **and** *he intended to make her pay.* (p. 108)

The lotus garden was lit only by starlight, **and** *the air was warm and smelled of stagnant water.* (p. 132)

She was wearing a fine black dress with jet beads sewn on the front, **and** *Matt thought she looked strange without her apron.* (p. 151)

—Nancy Farmer, *The House of the Scorpion*

LESSON

From Splice to Nice—FANBOYS to the Rescue

I retype a few sentences from a novel like *The House of the Scorpion,* deleting the coordinating conjunctions. As a class we study the sentences, identifying each sentence's two subjects and two verbs. We talk about the commas, and before you know it, someone points out the missing conjunctions. I walk over to the compound sentence wall chart, if no one else mentions it, and connect the students' words and questions to the graphic representation of the compound sentence pattern. As writers, I ask them to help me choose the best FANBOYS for the job in each sentence, letting students insert the new coordinating conjunctions and discussing them together. "Which one sounds better? Why?" The craft of writing is our subject, meaning and effect our goals.

We work on adding compound sentences to our writer's notebook collections. Invariably, a sharp-eyed student will find an intentional comma splice in published writing. When that happens, the student writes the spliced sentence on a transparency and we look at it as a class, even if it means interrupting writing time. Instead of an exception being a stumbling block, we discover the variation as a choice that has effects, and knowing how to correct it for standard form gives the students a sense of power. "This is in a published book that professional editors and writers have gone over with a fine-toothed comb. Do you think they just missed this one? Why might an author 'break the rules' in this way? Does it work?"

We also discuss that, when writing for unknown or formal audiences, it would be best to avoid comma splices, intentional or not. For fun, we "correct" the sentence by replacing the comma with a semicolon or simply adding a coordinating conjunction. We talk about the different effects and vote on which ones we like. It's always a divided vote, whether the feelings are strong or not.

Visual Scaffold

Collecting Compound Sentences

Jaime collected these compound sentences from Megan McDonald's *Judy Moody Gets Famous!* (2003) and Joan Lowery Nixon's *Shadowmaker* (1994).

<u>Judy Moody Gets Famous</u>

Jessica Aardwolf Finch might be famous, but she was also a silly old termite-eater. (7)

It was Almost time for science her best Subject, so it would be easy for Judy to pay Attention. (29)

<u>Shadow maker</u>

A few kids groaned, and one (134) asked if he could be excused because he had baseball pratice

2.3 No Comma After an Introductory Element

In Plain English   If a sentence begins with a phrase or clause or transition, you probably need a comma to separate it from the independent clause that follows. In other words, use a comma after an introduction or opener.

AKA   No comma after an opener, introductory phrase, subordinate or dependent clause, modifier, transition or transitional phrase.

The most common introductory word groups are clauses and phrases functioning as adverbs. Such word groups usually tell when, where, how, why, or under what conditions the main action of the sentence occurred. A comma tells readers that the introductory clause or phrase has come to a close and that the main part of the sentence is about to begin.
—Diana Hacker, *A Writer's Reference*

Commas after introductory elements or openers help readers understand how sentence parts are separated, cueing them as to how to read them aloud, and aiding them in making sense of the intended message. The principle of inserting a comma after an introductory element is a crucial one that is often tested on state exams, as well as applied by student writers.

Certain words can signal writers that a comma may be needed after the opener. When positioned as the first word of a sentence, signal words such as *after, since, if,* and *when* tell the writer a comma is probably needed.

Participles in the position of the first word also indicate that a comma will probably be needed. If sentences that begin with signal words don't have commas, students should be put on fragment alert. Often students are tested on fragments, which are merely clauses that begin with *-ing* verbs or subordinate conjunctions: *While I was gone; After the gold rush; If I can't have you.* All make effective titles or great sentence openers if attached to an independent clause. (See the Appendix for "AAAWWUBBIS and More!," a complete list of subordinating conjunctions; and "Comma Magnets as Sentence Openers," a list of other transitional words and adverbs that often serve as introductory elements or openers for sentences.

Student Error   *After chasing the ice cream truck two blocks Priscilla and I realized we didn't have any money.*

Behind the Error   When students make this error, I just assume I haven't taught the concept of using a comma after an opener in enough ways. After all, the fact that they're making ventures into complex sentences is a wonderful thing. A sentence including an introductory element is usually the first type of complex sentence that students will try without prompting.

Mentor Text   **If** you can't annoy somebody, *there is little point in writing.*
—Kingsley Amis, *The King's English*

When summer comes to the North Woods, *time slows down.* (p. 1)
—Jennifer Donnelly, *A Northern Light*

When I saw the woman, *she reminded me of a bird.* **Though** her hair was white with age, *she walked with small, quick, lively steps.* (p. 13)
—Laurence Yep, *The Star Fisher*

Looking back on it now, *I doubt that there was any way I could have imagined what lay ahead.* (p. 3)
—James Howe, *Howliday Inn*

Holding his hat against his chest and Tartufo's leash with one hand, *he knocked on his office door with the other.* (p. 6)
—E. L. Konigsburg, *The Outcasts of 19 Schuyler Place*

If There Were an Olympic Contest for Sentence Imitating

I put this sentence from *Flipped* (2001) on the overhead: *If there was an Olympic contest for talking, Shelly Stalls would sweep the event* (p. 16). Students always love this sentence, and it's a breeze to imitate its structure.

I share with the students that one way we can learn to craft sentences is to imitate those of favorite authors. With warnings beforehand against cruelty, we spend some time rewriting this sentence, filling in the blanks: *If there were an Olympic contest for _____, _____ would sweep the event.* Jericha came up with this imitation: *If there were an Olympic contest for eating, my brother would sweep the event.*

In my mind, if there were an Olympic contest for best sentence to imitate, this one would sweep the event.

AAAWWUBBIS—The Subordinating Conjunction Bionic Mnemonic

AAAWWUBBIS is a mnemonic used to help students remember the subordinating conjunctions: *after, although, as, when, while, until, because, before, if, since.* But I don't tell the kids that. I just write the term on the wall chart and start using it—seeing whether they can figure it out. It at least builds up some curiosity.

"Sir, what's that?" someone asks.

"It's an Ah-whoo-bus!" I hoot. "When your sentence begins with an AAAWWUBBIS, you're probably going to need a comma somewhere in there." In general, when I say this, especially when I really whoop up AAAWWUBBIS, it gets my students' attention. I explain how they already know AAAWWUBBIS. I remind them of the book *When I Was Little* (1993), which we read to generate ideas for a personal essay about our own childhoods. We discuss how Jamie Lee Curtis uses a comma after every single *When I was little.*

The students practice using the pattern, starting every sentence about their past with *When I was little.* "What do you need after *When I was little*?" I ask. "You have seven minutes to list all the *When I was little* sentences you can." After we list, we do a buddy check, ensuring that each writer put a comma after every *When I was little.* Next, students pick one or a few ideas that are related and freewrite. But, before students start writing, I reveal what an AAAWWUBBIS is. AAAWWUBBIS is the mnemonic for the subordinating conjunctions (*although, after, as, when, while, unless, before, because, if, since*), but it's more fun to yell AAAWWUBBIS! I let them have lots of oral practice using them, saying the comma aloud. After saying them orally, they start writing and use as many as they can.

Visual Scaffold

Teacher Model of *When I Was Little* Listing Activity

I model using the *When I was little* clause in front of each item on my list, modeling the comma placement as well.

> When I was little, I had a tree house, which was really just a piece of
>   plywood my dad nailed up in the chinaberry tree.
> When I was little, I ate cold Spaghetti-O's right out of the can.
> When I was little, I watched *The Brady Bunch,* but I thought it was *The Grady
>   Bunch.*
> When I was little, I called the disposal, the suppose-all.
> When I was little, I didn't always hear things right, so I didn't say things right.
> When I was little, I used to run around without my shirt or shoes all summer
>   long.
> When I was little, I used to walk to school with my *Partridge Family* lunch kit
>   swinging by my side.

Opener Pattern Graphic

I borrowed the term *opener* from Don Killgallon (1998) to simplify *introductory element.* Graphic representation allows for many different kinds of openers (single words, phrases, or clauses). A reproducible version of this graphic is included in "Three Basic Complex Sentence Pattern Visual Scaffolds" in the Appendix.

Use a comma to set off an **opener.**

Opener **,** **sentence** **.**

AAAWWUBBIS Poster

Joshua points to the subordinating conjunctions' mnemonic to remind the class why his sentence needs a comma.

2.4 No Comma in a Nonrestrictive Element

OPERATOR'S MANUAL

In Plain English   When a group of words interrupts a sentence, it needs to have commas on both sides. Use two commas to set off nonessential information.

AKA   No comma setting off nonessential information. Nonrestrictive elements may also be known as appositives, asides, parentheticals, or adjectives out of order (Noden 1999).

Interrupters, or embedded details, add information to a sentence. The interrupter sentence pattern gives the writer the option of adding information, a sort of double exposure of the preceding noun, which provides the reader with more details about it. Sometimes writers want to add an aside to a sentence, to use the grammatical equivalent of cupped hands to add parenthetical embedded details. When I introduce interrupters to kids, I start by lifting and separating a sentence with an interrupter, such as this one from *Summer of the Monkeys* by Wilson Rawls (1998):

> *, my bluetick hound,*
> I even coaxed Rowdy   into helping me
> with this monkey trouble. (p. 1)

Is it still a complete sentence without the information *my bluetick hound*? *I even coaxed Rowdy into helping me with this monkey trouble*. It's still a sentence. It's a nice detail to know what kind of dog Rowdy is. It may even make a picture in our heads, but it is not grammatically necessary. But some may argue that it's essential to know Rowdy is a dog: *I even coaxed my dog Rowdy into helping me with this monkey trouble*. Some may argue that it is the positioning of *my bluetick hound* in the interrupter sentence pattern that causes the need for the commas. The interrupter, in this case an appositive, renames Rowdy. An interrupter often clarifies the noun in front of it, but if it is to be set off with commas, the interrupter shouldn't be essential to the meaning of the sentence. It should be noted that this is an oversimplification. But I have learned that oversimplification with students is often necessary at the beginning of concept development.

Let's save deciding whether a phrase is restrictive or nonrestrictive (essential or nonessential) for later. It makes my head hurt, and I wish I didn't have to mention it at all. Even editor Constance Hale (1999) says grappling with this distinction is only for "a real grammar masochist" (p. 173). The error of leaving off the comma is many times more frequent than that of unnecessarily setting off a phrase with a comma or commas. In general, if the sentence can still be a sentence without the information, the added information is nonessential and needs to be set off with a comma or commas.

Student Error   *Usher a real fine guy, sings so sweet.*

Behind the Error   Sabrina has an idea to use commas to set off the interrupters and understands that the interrupters can rename a noun. She is getting a sense that there are ways to combine thoughts in one sentence. This is a gateway that kids pass through, usually with more mistakes than when they previously wrote simple sentences.

Mentor Text

*I was stretched out on my back, **my paws dangling at my sides,** thinking nothing more of the meal I'd just eaten and the chocolate I hoped still lie ahead.* (p. 3)
*Only Howie, **who was growling as he chewed vigorously on a rawhide bone,** seemed unable to relax.* (p. 4)
—James Howe, *The Celery Stalks at Midnight*

*And she didn't want to sit next to Frank Pearl, **who ate paste,** in class.* (p. 9)
—Megan McDonald, *Judy Moody*

*Intricate mosaic tiles, **handpicked by Baba in Isfahan,** covered the four floors of the four bathrooms.* (p. 4)
—Khaled Hosseini, *The Kite Runner*

LESSON

Basket Case—The Essential Nonessential Comma Rule

I put a sentence from *The Celery Stalks at Midnight* (2002) on the overhead: *I was stretched out on my back, **my paws dangling at my sides,** thinking nothing more of the meal I'd just eaten and the chocolate I hoped still lie ahead.* "Pretend that the commas around **my paws dangling at my sides** are like basket handles," I say. I explain that if I can lift out the clause and still have a sentence, then it's nonessential, and I need to put commas around both sides. "When I lift and separate the interrupter, we're left with *I was stretched out on my back thinking nothing more of the meal I'd just eaten and the chocolate I hoped still lie ahead.*" I explain how I will insert a new comma to set off this *-ing* clause at the end of the sentence. "Is it still a sentence? So, commas are needed."

Students come up to the overhead and do more sentences, soliciting help from their classmates, tying them back to the visual scaffold.

As a craft move, we explore how this is like adding a comma zoom lens to writing. Looking again at the sentences with the interrupters, we close our eyes and try to picture them, discussing how the interrupters add little close-up pictures for our eyes to see. "Making mind movies is an author's job," I remind them, "so we have something to see in our minds. Interrupters can also help us combine two sentences by embedding the information from one sentence in the other."

LESSON

An Appositive Imitation Is the Sincerest Form of Flattery . . . But Plagiarism Isn't

For more practice, I give students a sentence to imitate, a sentence that will show them how the interrupter can be as simple as a word or phrase that renames the subject (an appositive). Before we start, we discuss how we imitate structure, not content, and the other differences between imitation and plagiarism. We imitate the following sentence from *She's Come Undone* by Wally Lamb (1998):

> *Our yellow ranch house, **26 Bobolink Drive,** had a garage and a bathroom shower with sliding glass doors.* (p. 18)

I show them my imitation, which mimics the structure but not the content. We check our sentences with the basket test.

*Our new apartment, **Number 24 in The Pierre Marquis,** had green shag carpeting you had to rake and a rented couch in the living room. The locks worked well, too. That's what I learned that day I forgot my key.*

We try another from Hosseini's *The Kite Runner*:

*Intricate mosaic tiles, **handpicked by Baba in Isfahan,** covered the four floors of the four bathrooms.* (p. 4)

Again, I show them my imitation, which includes a bonus appositive in the closer position:

*Colorful peel and stick tiles, **handpicked by Darlene at Home Depot,** covered the floor of the one and only bathroom she shared with her four younger brothers—**four filthy barefoot heathens.** At least that's what her mother called them.*

If these imitations make us want to write, we go with it, knowing that imitation takes us someplace new. Here is a sentence from *Cuba 15* by Nancy Osa (2005), with another appositive in the closer position, and our imitation:

*Mom ran the Rise & Walk Thrift Sanctuary, **a used-clothing shop in the church basement that operates on donations.*** (p. 2)

*Mom owned a Century 21, **a makeshift real estate office in a former swimming pool retail store.** A pool sat right outside her office.*

Visual Scaffold　　**Interrupter Sentence Pattern**

The term *interrupter* covers any sentence part that could be inserted into a sentence, and which must be set off with commas. A reproducible version of this graphic is included in "Three Basic Complex Sentence Pattern Visual Scaffolds" in the Appendix.

Use two commas to set off an **interrupter.**

Her hair, **brown and flowing,** was held back with a scrunchy.

Mr. Talk, **our English teacher,** says we're intelligent.

2.5 No Comma Setting Off Additions at the End of a Sentence

OPERATOR'S MANUAL

In Plain English Use a comma to set off additional information if it's after an independent clause and the additions modify or describe elements of the clause.

AKA Run-on, closer, cumulative sentence.

Sentences move in a direction, whether through description or narration. In cases of narration and description, the writer attempts to show things as they appear through close observation, with verbs that show the action for narration and nouns that show concrete details for description. When writing a sentence, a writer has the tools of nouns or verbs to convey his or her observations. Look at this sentence from *Bud, Not Buddy* by Christopher Paul Curtis (2000):

> All the other kids watched the woman as she moved along the line, **her high-heeled shoes sounding like firecrackers going off on the wooden floor.**
> (p. 1)

The base clause of the sentence (*All the other kids watched the woman as she moved along the line*) gives us a wide-angle shot of kids watching a woman, and then the sentence moves to the concreteness of nouns, setting off our senses of hearing and seeing (*her high-heeled shoes sounding like firecrackers going off on the wooden floor*).

Even the adjectives in this sentence are noun-ish (high-heeled, wooden), naming things that we can see or have heard before. The *closer* of this sentence adds sensory detail that modifies the base clause, creating a perfect cumulative sentence, pulling our eyes into a close-up on the high-heels, not only visually, but aurally as well. Christensen (1968) thought that the cumulative sentence was the one type of sentence English teachers could best spend their time teaching, because of the closer's ability to ground our sentences in the concrete and the ease with which students can add free modifiers.

More recently, Noden has shown us how free modifiers, such as absolutes, can add close-up images and actions to many sentences, describing the comma as a zoom lens that affords us the privilege of seeing parts of the base clause up close and personal. Teaching our students from time to time to write cumulative sentences describing things they observe can crack open the kids' writing at a more concrete level, giving reason and purpose to their use of commas to "chunk" sentences meaningfully and intentionally as well as to zoom in on detail.

Student Error *It was time to get my haircut bangs over my eyes flopping back down every time I brush it back.*

Behind the Error At first glance, this sentence seems much more problematic than it is. Though it appears to be a run-on sentence, closer examination reveals that all the additions at the close of the sentence go back to modify or sharpen the image introduced in the base clause: *It was time to get my haircut.* Eric has stumbled on the absolute (bangs over my eyes) and a participial phrase (flopping back down every time I brush it back). The sentence just needs to be separated into meaningful chunks: *It was time to get my haircut, bangs over my eyes flopping back down every time I brush my hair back.*

Mentor Text *The screen was coming away from the screen door in one corner, **curling away from the metal frame like a leaf.** The volume-control knob had fallen off the hi-fi, **leaving a forked metal bud.** (p. 59)*
—Suzanne Berne, *A Crime in the Neighborhood*

*There was a lot of posing going on, **a kind of auditioning or something.** (p. 156)*
—Francesca Lia Block, *The Rose and the Beast*

*The massive thighs, which emerged from out of the smock, were encased in a pair of extraordinary trousers, **bottle-green in color and made of course twill.** (p. 83)*
—Roald Dahl, *Matilda*

*I became what I am today at the age of twelve, on a frigid overcast day in the winter of 1975. I remember the precise moment, **crouching behind the crumbling mud wall, peeking into the alley near the frozen creek.** That was a long time ago, but it's wrong what they say about the past, I've learned, about how you can bury it. Because the past claws its way out. Looking back now, I realize I have been peaking into the deserted alley for the last twenty-six years. (p. 1)*
—Khaled Hosseini, *The Kite Runner*

Life Detectives—Paying Attention to Detail and the Cumulative Sentence

First, we talk about the writer's craft of close observation by reading aloud *The Other Way of Listening* by Byrd Baylor (1997). This picture book tells a story of learning to observe, to sense things not everyone senses. The book sparks conversation about other ways of listening and seeing the world around us. Later, I take a few paragraphs from Louise Fitzhugh's *Harriet the Spy* for younger students or Suzanne Berne's *Crime in the Neighborhood* (1998) for older students. This keystone of writer's craft, close observation, will be the wellspring of students' need for grammar and use of grammar to aid their thinking and observation. Here is a useful passage from Berne's book:

> *The trick, I realized, was to notice everything.*
>
> *And so it was that the day after Mr. Green, our new neighbor moved in, I began keeping a notebook in which I documented the travels through my house. I noted the worn patches in the hallway's oriental runner, the scuff marks on the stairs, the scorch at the back of the lampshade in the living room. The screen was coming away from the screen door in one corner, **curling away from the metal frame like a leaf.** The volume-control knob had fallen off the hi-fi, **leaving a forked metal bud.** Steven had spilled India ink on the sofa, and if you turned over the left cushion, you found a deep blue stain shaped like a moose antler. I had never noticed our house contained so many damaged things. Soon it seemed I couldn't look at anything without finding something wrong with it.*
>
> *On the cover of my notebook, I wrote "Evidence." (p. 59)*

For a homework assignment or perhaps a silent-observation walk, I encourage kids to find something they can observe and describe. Students don't have to observe people, but they do need to observe closely, whether it's at the bus stop or the grocery store or the cafeteria or the dining room table. They must describe what they see. Once students have collected their field notes, I model an observation of my dog Ellen.

*Ellen plops down in the middle of the floor, **her body angled toward me, eyes blinking, then gives a long moan as she lays down on her side, legs crossed, eyes closed.***

I explain that though I set out to describe Ellen, observing her movements led me into a narrative sentence. I go back and add *hardwood* in front of *floor*. "Let's look at what I did," I say. "First, I wrote a base sentence: *Ellen plops down in the middle of the floor.*" I describe how I added close-ups to my sentence by adding the things I saw and heard, in a narrative progression, following their progression in time.

Students then try to write a base sentence. We make sure this is correct with a buddy check because it is so crucial to have this base sentence for all our modifiers to lean on, to circle back to with concrete description and narration. Next we look at my additions, talking about structure and possibility, depending on what kind of sentence parts we have discussed so far. (See "Comma Reinforcers" in the Appendix.)

Visual Scaffold

Make Sentences Concrete With Sensory Detail
Students can periodically choose one or two sensory detail closers.

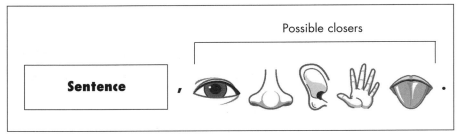

Closer Sentence Pattern
A reproducible version of this graphic is included in "Three Basic Complex Sentence Pattern Visual Scaffolds" in the Appendix.

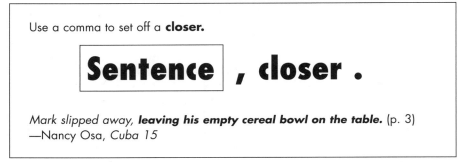

Use a comma to set off a **closer.**

Sentence , **closer** .

*Mark slipped away, **leaving his empty cereal bowl on the table.*** (p. 3)
—Nancy Osa, *Cuba 15*

2.6 Lack of Commas in a Series

OPERATOR'S MANUAL

In Plain English   Use commas to separate a series of three or more things, actions, or phrases. Commas in a series separate items or actions so the reader can identify each intended item. In other words, use commas as separators to keep the items or actions in discrete chunks and to ease communication.

AKA   Missing serial commas or listing commas.

Look at the following examples of commas used in a series:

> I love to eat **apples, bananas, and grapefruits.**

> **Getting** to school on time, **doing** all my assignments, and **behaving** well are all things I can do to ensure my success in school.

Some newspaper editors, lawyers, and many a picky English teacher want to see the final comma before the *and* or *or*. Atwell (1998) calls it the Harvard comma. It's been called the Oxford comma as well. My thoughts: Why not use it? Yes, you don't have to, but you might be judged if you don't. And you will never be wrong if you put that comma before the last item.

The idea of balance or parallelism is particularly important to the craft of making good lists: Nouns go with nouns, verbs with verbs, and adverbs with adverbs. Words joined by *and* should always be parallel. And if your list is a list of actions, make sure that they are equal and start in the same way. In this excerpt from *Slave Day* (1998), notice how Rob Thomas uses a present tense verb at the start of each of his phrases in the list:

> With a malicious gleam in his eye, he **kicks** back the chair, **pulls** out his shirt tails, **and adopts** the high-volume grunting and braying tones of a Mississippi Delta evangelist. (p. 1)

Student Error   *My Aunt Chula Uncle Vince and all my cousins went down to the river to swim.*

Behind the Error   Valerie may have just been writing so fast that she forgot to use commas to separate the people who went down to the river.

Mentor Text   *The soup was a masterwork, a delicate mingling of **chicken, watercress, and garlic.** (p. 110)*
*Can you imagine your father selling you for **a tablecloth, a hen, and a handful of cigarettes**? Close your eyes, please, and consider it for just a moment.*
Done?
I hope that the hair on your back of your neck stood up as you thought of Mig's fate and how it would be if it were your own. (p. 127)
—Kate DiCamillo, The Tale of Despereaux

Sometimes authors leave out the coordinating conjunction before the last item for a staccato effect:

> *What I wasn't used to was having his smell back,* **the smoke from his Camel cigarettes, his Old Spice aftershave, the shoe polish he used on his boots.** *All those father odors, filling up the house. My mother* **opened every window, waxed the wooden furniture, sprayed room freshener in every corner.** *She* **scrubbed the tiles on the bathroom floor, scrubbed the dog's water bowl, scrubbed her hair, her hands, her face,** *shiny. Then she sat in her convertible and wept it all away, all but the smell. "I can't scrub the air," she said. And so he was there, but not really. Where was he?* (p. 29)
> —Kathi Appelt, *My Father's Summers*

Think-Aloud—Commas, Are You Serial?

I begin with, "I want you to listen to me say a sentence: *I don't like rap, but I do like Outcast, Eminem, Black-Eyed Peas.* Does it make sense?" I put the sentence on the overhead without the commas in a series: *I don't like rap, but I do like Outcast Eminem Black-Eyed Peas.*

We discuss how, without any commas, the sentence makes it look like Outcast, Eminem, and the Black-Eyed Peas are *one* thing. There are five comma rules students need to know to survive sentences, and this is one of them. "I know that, when I am writing a list of three or more items, I have to put a comma after each item in the list, except the last one. I also usually need to use *and* or *or* before the last item."

We look at the wall chart and see how this looks graphically. Then we look at a mentor text on the overhead such as this one from Kate DiCamillo's *The Tale of Despereaux*: *Can you imagine your father selling you for a tablecloth, a hen, and a handful of cigarettes?* Then, looking back at my sentence, a student tells me where to add the commas. I point out how the commas help each item keep its own identity, doing what separators do best: *I don't like rap, but I do like Outcast, Eminem, and Black-Eyed Peas.* "I know to pause each time I see a comma; that's what punctuation does. It tells us how to read the words around the marks," I explain.

Next, we discuss how this pattern works with a series of actions as well by looking at an excerpt from Kathi Appelt's *My Father's Summers,* in which the author so adeptly evokes the underused sense of smell: *My mother opened every window, waxed the wooden furniture, sprayed room freshener in every corner. She scrubbed the tiles on the bathroom floor, scrubbed the dog's water bowl, scrubbed her hair, her hands, her face, shiny.* The kids notice how there isn't an *and* before the last item. We talk about the effect and look at another example from Appelt: *What I wasn't used to was having his smell back, the smoke from his Camel cigarettes, his Old Spice aftershave, the shoe polish he used on his boots.* We add in *and* and discuss how it is an option to leave out the *and* but how, in more formal situations or in questions on tests, they should follow the principle of using the conjunction before the last item.

To apply the idea to our own writing, we write a few sentences about ourselves or something we've observed in our writer's notebooks, using serial commas in various ways. Later, we will do a buddy check and share a few of our sentences.

Visual Scaffold

Categorizing Serial Comma Sentences

To begin sentence collecting, students hunt for serial comma sentences in texts and record them on small strips of paper. If a wrong sentence gets on the chart, we look at the sentence as a class and see why it fooled someone.

Serial Comma Sentence Pattern

When students read for meaning, they start to see it's not about having commas in a sentence, it's about what the commas do to the sentence. A reproducible version of this scaffold is included in "Compound and Serial Comma Sentence Pattern Scaffolds" in the Appendix.

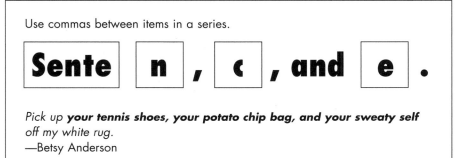

Use commas between items in a series.

Sente **n** **,** **c** **, and** **e** **.**

*Pick up **your tennis shoes, your potato chip bag, and your sweaty self** off my white rug.*
—Betsy Anderson

Pronouns:
The Willing Stand-Ins

*The pronoun is a useful little part of speech that resembles a
World War II minefield when it comes to error possibilities.*

> Geraldine Woods, *English Grammar for Dummies*

*The use of male pronouns as the gender-neutral default is a dying
tradition, but that problem is easier said than solved.*

> Bill Walsh, *The Elephants of Style*

The battle between whose *and* who's *comes up less frequently
than the one between* its *and* it's, *but the problems are identical.
If you can solve one, you've got the other one whipped.*

> Patricia O'Conner, *Woe Is I*

It, *clearly a pronoun meant to refer to an idea previously
expressed, is often used by students to refer to an idea still in
their heads.*
Joyce Armstrong Carroll and Edward E. Wilson, *Acts of Teaching*

*What should you say on the phone: "It is me?" or "It is I?"
Maybe you should just hang up the phone and send a fax.*
Laurie E. Rozakis, *The Complete Idiot's Guide to Grammar and Style*

3.1 Vague Pronoun Reference

OPERATOR'S MANUAL

In Plain English   If the reader can't tell which word(s) a pronoun **refer**s to (the antecedent), that makes a vague pronoun **refer**ence. Pronouns (*pro* meaning "for") stand in for nouns, keeping writing succinct and less repetitive. What a pronoun replaces has to be easy for the reader to see. Pronouns also establish the point of view of the narrator.

AKA   No clear pronoun reference, lack of pronoun antecedents, obscure pronominal reference.

Your biggest problems with pronouns will come if you lose sight of the antecedent: when a pronoun drifts away from its antecedent, the entire meaning gets lost at sea.
—Constance Hale, *Sin and Syntax*

In a craft sense, pronouns set the tone of our writing by establishing a point of view:

- **First person** (*I, we* voice): The first-person point of view lets the narrator be a central part of the story, allowing readers to feel the immediacy of events and feelings.
- **Second person** (*you* voice): The second-person point of view involves the reader in the story or article almost conversationally, as an accomplice, as part of the thinking or judgment. Using the you point of view is hard to pull off in longer pieces. (See *Loser* by Spinelli, *You Don't Know Me* by David Klass, and any book by Chuck Palahniuk.)
- **Third person** (*he, she, it, they* voice): The third-person point of view can give the reader a sense that the writer is removed from his or her subject. In nonfiction, the third-person point of view helps the writer maintain objectivity. In fiction, the third-person omniscient allows the author to see inside all characters' thoughts without being a character in the story. Third-person limited allows the author to see inside only one character's thoughts. When writing about a memory that is difficult, sometimes shifting to third-person observation allows writers to get the writing down, and it may be a better way to tell an important story.

Student Error   *We ate at McDonald's for breakfast, it was delicious. I got a breakfast biscuit, hash browns, and orange juice. It looked beautiful, it had a picture. That had dolphins and sharks and fish. It was really nice inside McDonald's.*

Behind the Error   Clearly Ashley has made the "it parade," what O'Conner refers to as a "pronoun pileup" (p. 68). It's just not clear what *it* is—and there are many vague *its* to choose from. Ashley believes we know what she means (perhaps we do), but this same problem plagues many writers. Reiterating the idea of proximity, which comes up with many clarity issues, is the key.

Mentor Text   *The sweet-shop . . . was the very centre of our lives. To us, it was what a bar is to a drunk, or a church to a Bishop. Without it, there would have been little to live for. But it had one terrible drawback, this sweet-shop. The woman who owned it was a horror. We hated her and had good reason for doing so.*

   Her name was Mrs. Pratchett. She was a small skinny old hag with a moustache on her upper lip. . . . She never smiled. She never welcomed us when we went in, and the only times she spoke were when she had said things like, "I'm watchin' you so keep your thievin' fingers off them chocolates!" Or "I don't want you in 'ere just to look around! Either you forks *out or you* gets *out!*

But by far the most loathsome thing about Mrs. Pratchett was the filth that clung around her. Her apron was grey and greasy. Her blouse had bits of breakfast all over it, toast-crumbs and tea stains and splotches of dead egg-yolk. It was her hands, however, that disturbed us most. They were disgusting. They were black with dirt and grime. (pp. 34–35)
—Roald Dahl, *Boy: Tales of Childhood*

In his book of humorous grammar errors, *Anguished English* (1989), Richard Lederer includes this gem of what *not* to do, which he found in a church bulletin:

The ladies of the church have cast off clothing of every kind, and they can be seen in the church basement Friday afternoon. (p. 44)

Marking Text—In Reference to Pronouns

I give students a triple-spaced copy of the excerpt from Roald Dahl's *Boy: Tales of Childhood*. Students discover when a story is told in the *I/we* voice (first person) that there may be no referent, except the narrator.

Prior to this, I have read an extension of this passage aloud to my students and had them do a freewrite about where they buy candy or a store clerk. I like to use shared texts like this in several ways.

"A few days ago we read this passage from Roald Dahl's memoir *Boy*," I begin. In pairs, students do some rereading because though the other day Mr. Dahl taught us about showing instead of telling, we can still learn more from him.

"When Dahl uses pronouns like *he, she, it, we,* and *us,* readers can tell what he is referring to. Sometimes writers use pronouns that don't have clear antecedents," I say. We discuss that *antecedent* means some word had to come before this pronoun to make it a pronoun proper. Sometimes linking the word *antecedent* to ancestors helps kids remember that the antecedent comes *before* and is necessary. "All that means is, if you use an *it* or a *she,* the reader should be able to tell who or what the pronoun is referring to, or the pronoun referent."

I say to the students, "Let's look at Dahl's first few sentences as a class. First let's find the pronouns and highlight them."

*The sweet-shop in Llandaff in the year 1923 was the very centre of our lives. To **us, it** was what a bar is to a drunk, or a church to a Bishop. Without **it,** there would have been little to live for. But **it** had one terrible drawback, this sweet-shop. The woman who owned **it** was a horror. **We** hated **her** and had good reason for doing so.*

We discuss what the pronouns refer to, how we can tell, and whether the references are clear. I model by drawing an arrow back to the antecedent. "Let's draw a line with an arrow from *it* to *sweet-shop* to show what *it* is referring to. More *its,* oh, so all of the *its* go back to the *sweet-shop.* Let's make sure."

With a partner, students continue highlighting each pronoun and drawing an arrow to its antecedent. About halfway through the assignment, we stop and discuss our progress as a class, working through any confusion.

Afterward, students look back at the piece they have already written in response to reading the Dahl excerpt the first time, checking for vague pronoun references by highlighting pronouns and drawing highlight arrows back to the antecedents. This is followed by buddy checking and sharing what they discovered about pronoun reference.

For more pronoun fun, see "More Than Anyone Wants to Know About Pronouns" in the Appendix.

Visual Scaffold

Connecting Pronouns to Their Antecedents.

In groups, students find pronouns and put boxes around them. Then, students draw arrows back to whatever the pronouns are referring to (their antecedents).

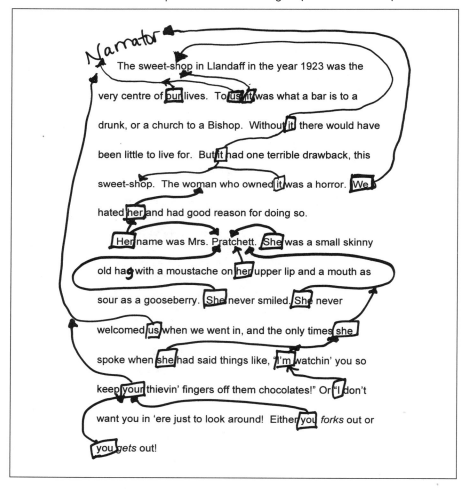

3.2 Pronoun-Antecedent Agreement Error

OPERATOR'S MANUAL

In Plain English   Pronoun agreement error is a mismatch between the pronoun and its antecedent, involving gender, number, or person.

AKA   Pronoun reference error, antecedent error.

Pronouns and their antecedents were made for each other.
—Karen Elizabeth Gordon, *The Deluxe Intransitive Vampire*

Though there are some disagreements about pronoun-antecedent agreement, a few principles stand firm. As a craft issue, this error can distract the reader from the message or put into question the writer's reliability as a source.

First, your pronoun should match the gender of its antecedent. Use *he, his,* and *him* for the menfolk; *she* and *her* for the womenfolk; and *it* for the inanimate objects or entities. The following is an example of an agreement error involving gender:

> *We loved Donna, and he loved us.*

Unless Donna had a mother with a twisted sense of humor, Donna is a she. That's agreeing in gender.

Next, writers' pronouns and antecedents need to match in number. Writers match plural antecedents with plural pronouns and singular antecedents with singular pronouns. Here is an example of an agreement error involving number:

> *We loved Donna, and she loved me.*

We can't become a "me" (unless someone leaves us for being so obsessed with grammar). **We** *loved Donna, and she loved* **us**. That's agreeing in number. And it would be that simple, if it weren't for indefinite pronouns such as these:

- **Singular:** *another, anybody, anyone, anything, each, either, everybody, everyone, everything, little, much, neither, nobody, no one, nothing, one, other, somebody, someone, something*
- **Plural:** *both, few, many, others, several*
- **Singular or Plural:** *all, any, more, most, none, some* (It depends on what noun it refers to: *none of the students* would be plural and *more time* would be singular.)

When we use a pronoun after a singular indefinite pronoun, we can either make the genders costar (*Each of the students keeps his or her writer's notebook in the classroom*), or recast our sentences with plural antecedents (*The students keep their writer's notebooks in the classroom*). Using only male pronouns is considered sexist, so, whenever possible, we should be gender inclusive. Changing single subjects like *student* to *students* when possible will save you from this problem. Recasting your sentence altogether may alleviate the problem as well. See the Web site of the National Council of Teachers of English (NCTE) for current guidelines on nonsexist language (ncte.org or http://www.ncte.org/about/over/positions/category/lang/107647.htm).

When antecedents are considered one entity, they take a singular pronoun. We write *The administration lost its control of the teachers,* not *The administration lost their control of the teachers.* Collective nouns that should be considered as one entity, such as *the government, a company, the administration,* or *a class,* take singular pronouns.

Student Error   *The substitute, who was angry, told the class to do whatever they wanted.*

Behind the Error   The thinking about this error is not difficult to see. A *class* is more than one person, and plural means more than one, so logically Samantha used a plural pronoun. She has a clear antecedent and made a mistake based on patterns she knows and patterns she hears in spoken language. While this error is not so frowned on in speech, it can be in formal writing. The idea of collective entities being considered singular will need to be introduced so that Samantha will understand why she should use the singular pronoun *it* when referring to an antecedent such as *class.*

Mentor Text   *My sister, Lynn, taught me my first word: kira-kira. I pronounced it ka-a-ahhh, but she knew what I meant. Kira-kira means "glittering" in Japanese. Lynn told me that when I was a baby, she used to take me onto our empty road at night, where we would lie on our backs and look at the stars while she said over and over, "Katie, say 'kira-kira, kira-kira." I loved that word! When I grew older, I used kira-kira to describe everything I liked: the beautiful blue sky, puppies, kittens, butterflies, colored Kleenex.*

My mother said we were misusing the word; you could not call a Kleenex kira-kira. She was dismayed over how un-Japanese we were and vowed to send us to Japan one day. I didn't care where she sent me as long as Lynn came along. (pp. 1–2)
—Cynthia Kadohata, *Kira-Kira*

LESSON

Where Have All the Pronouns Gone? A *Kira-Kira* Cloze

I like to use the mentor text *Kira-Kira* with many of the pronouns removed (a reproducible version is included in the Appendix):

> _____ sister, Lynn, taught me _____ first word: kira-kira. I pronounced _____ ka-a-ahhh, but _____ knew what I meant. Kira-kira means "glittering" in Japanese. Lynn told _____ that when I was a baby, _____ used to take me onto our empty road at night, where we would lie on _____ backs and look at the stars while she said over and over, "Katie, say 'kira-kira, kira-kira'." _____ loved that word! When I grew older, _____ used kira-kira to describe _____ I liked: the beautiful blue sky, puppies, kittens, butterflies, colored Kleenex.
>
> My mother said _____ were misusing the word; you could not call a Kleenex kira-kira. _____ was dismayed over how un-Japanese we were and vowed to send _____ to Japan one day. I didn't care where she sent me, so long as Lynn came along.

I give the students the pronouns I removed on little bits of paper in an envelope, and students sort and categorize them. After they categorize the pronouns, I distribute the text with the removed pronouns and in groups they use context and antecedents to insert the pronouns in the proper places. After we share a few filled-in paragraphs, I pass out the original text, and we compare ours to it. A slight variation is to give students the passage with the removed pronouns and have them fill them in with whatever makes sense to them, using the "Pronoun Case Chart" found in the Appendix.

Visual Scaffold

Sort and Place
Group members sort verbs and place them into a *Kira-Kira* passage.

3.3 Pronoun Case Error

In Plain English

A pronoun can stand in for another noun to cut down on repetition. Whereas the vague pronoun reference error was all about clarity, and the pronoun-antecedent agreement error was all about number and person, the pronoun case error is all about function and placement in the sentence. Is the word acting as a subject, a possessive, or an object?

AKA

Nominative, objective, or possessive case errors.

Remember the most common pronoun-antecedent error happens when writers use they instead of it when referring to a singular body.
—Constance Hale, *Sin and Syntax*

Pronoun case is another case (pardon the pun) of dialectical difference. When I am reading Christopher Paul Curtis's Newbery Award-winning book *Bud, Not Buddy,* I am not taken aback when the narrator uses *me* at the beginning of a sentence as a subject. It's important that kids see this difference of purpose. In *Bud, Not Buddy,* Curtis is intentionally making a few dialectic choices to reflect the setting and life of his first-person narrator. This gives me a way to show how audience affects many choices we make as writers. "Maybe it's okay to say *Me and her went to the store* to your friends, but in more formal situations or registers, you need to understand what is considered Standard English: *She and I went to the store.*"

When teaching pronoun case to students, I keep a few tricks up my sleeve. These tips can be shared in a mini-lesson or a conference. Two tricks can help most kids out of most pronoun-case problems. First, if a pronoun is near the front of the sentence, it is likely to be in the subjective case: *I, we, you, he, she, it, they, this, that,* and *who.* If the pronoun is near the end of the sentence, it's probably in the objective case: *me, you, him, her, it, us, them, whom.* The chart in the visual scaffold mimics this positioning. And **to whom** it may concern, a pronoun that follows a preposition is always in the objective case.

Often students are perplexed at whether they should use *I* or *me* in their writing, or whether to use an apostrophe with their "itses." The pronoun case chart in the visual scaffold grounds us in the standard patterns of pronoun case; a reproducible "Pronoun Case Chart" with pronoun reminders is included in the Appendix.

Student Error

Me and Randy went to the store and bought some Lucas. Me and him ate the whole container, and, man it was good. Man, were we sick.

Behind the Error

Priscilla talks this way and so do her friends. It makes perfect sense to put yourself first in the sentence, you're speaking after all, but convention says the guest in her sentence should go first. (Then we have to deal with the fact that *me* is not correct usage when in either position.)

Mentor Text

*If **you** asked the kids and the teachers at Lincoln Elementary School to make three lists—all the really bad kids, all the really smart kids, and all the really good kids— Nick Allen would not be on any of **them.** Nick deserved a list all **his** own, and **everyone** knew it.*

*Was Nick a troublemaker? Hard to say. One thing's for sure: Nick Allen had plenty of ideas, and **he** knew how to use **them.***

*One time in third grade Nick decided to turn Mrs. Deaver's room into a tropical island. What kid in New Hampshire isn't ready for a little summer in February? So first **he** got everybody to make small palm trees out of green and brown construction paper and tape **them** onto the corners of each desk. Mrs. Deaver had only been a teacher for about six months, and **she** was delighted. "**That**'s so cute!"* (pp. 1–2)
—Andrew Clements, *Frindle*

*Is this the party **to whom** I am speaking?*
—Lily Tomlin as Ernestine

*You talkin' **to me**?*
—Robert De Niro in *Taxi Driver*

*Of all the gin joints in all the towns in all the world, she walks **into mine.***
—Humphrey Bogart in *Casablanca*

The Case of the Pesky Pronoun

I begin by talking about a student conference from the previous day. "Yesterday, Priscilla and I corrected a pronoun case error in her writing. I'll let Priscilla share a little trick with a wall chart we created." On the overhead Priscilla shows a sentence: *Me and Javier went to the holiday dance.* Priscilla says:

> *See, this sentence is good 'cause it's specific, but you want it to sound right, so here are a couple of tricks. First, you gotta remember you always let the guest in your sentence go first.* Javier and me went to the holiday dance. *Okay now, if you're confused about using* I *or* me *like I usually am, take away the guest and see how it sounds.*

Priscilla covers *Javier and* as I did when I modeled this in the conference. "*Me* went to the holiday dance. Now, I know that's wrong, so I have to use *I. Javier and I went to the holiday dance.*"

I follow by saying, "Priscilla taught you a good way to get your pronouns right:

- Put the guest first.
- Take away the guest to test your pronoun, and then put the guest back.

"Let's look at a paragraph from *Frindle* that's done correctly." I have bolded all the pronouns. "Let's discuss which case the words are and how we know they are correct."

For practice, I pass out slips of paper of some sentences that I have lifted from books or stories we have read, messing up the pronoun case. I ask buddies to help each other correct their slips:

> *Nick Allen had plenty of ideas, and him knew how to use it.*
> —Andrew Clements, *Frindle*

> *Every day after school since the beginning of sixth grade, me, Addie, Joe, and Skeezie have gathered at the Candy Kitchen, last booth on the right.*
> (p. 22)
> —James Howe, *The Misfits*

Kevin and me gawked at each other. (p. 6)
—Jerry Spinelli, *Stargirl*

Students work with partners to correct the sentences and make sure they have a rationale beyond the old standby, "I don't know; it sounds right." After we share the sentences and discuss the whys and hows, I challenge them to write a few mistakes and see whether their partners can get them corrected.

After this, I send students back into their own writing to do an express-lane edit on pronoun case. First they code the pronouns with a highlighter and then check case, using the tricks that they learned in the lesson. If someone gets stuck, we write the sentence on an overhead and have the class help him or her solve the problem. To keep cycling in this skill, I also make it into a game. When I read a sentence in *Because of Winn-Dixie* that uses non-Standard English, I ask the kids, "How could we say this sentence in Standard English?" They love it.

Visual Scaffold

Pronoun Case Chart
The visual organization helps students remember pronoun case more than calling each case by name (first person, second person, third person) does.

Pronoun Case		
Subjective	**Possessive**	**Objective**
I	my	me
you	your	you
he	his	him
she	her	her
it	its	it
we	our	us
they	their	them
who	whose	whom

Possessive Apostrophe Error

OPERATOR'S MANUAL

In Plain English   Use an apostrophe to show a contraction or to show ownership or possession. The apostrophe always communicates possession or contraction.

AKA   Confusion over homophones (spelling), possessives and contractions.

If you mix up your "itses" in front of a grammar stickler like Lynne Truss (author of *Eats, Shoots & Leaves*), she says, "You deserve to be struck by lightning, hacked up on the spot and buried in an unmarked grave" (p. 44). It's not hard to feel more tolerant than Ms. Truss, but really, I think the student's mix-up on this point is understandable and shows some grammatical prowess, however misapplied. The problem is, the two apostrophe rules step on each others' toes. Enter pronouns: They make these rules have exceptions. Take *it's* versus *its*. If I want to show possession, I show it with an apostrophe *s*, right? No! Even though the rule says to use an apostrophe to show possession, it works with everything but pronouns. Ah, the exceptions. I see the *it's* versus *its* error as part of a larger issue that can help with other big spelling problems (homophones). If writers can see the pattern, it can make a difference in how easily they can use the apostrophe appropriately.

Here's a handy *it's versus its* test: Can you replace the *it* with *it is*? Then use *it's*. If *it* is showing possession, then it's *its*. This test works for *who's* and *whose* too. *Who's* is short for *who is* and *whose* indicates *possession*. See the visual scaffold for other common homophones.

Student Error   *The dog chewed it's bone.*

Behind the Error   Perhaps Vanessa knows that apostrophes show possession, so she uses an apostrophe to show it's the dog's bone. The problem is, she is correct about the rule, but wrong in this case. She needs to see the larger patterns of this mechanics issue.

Mentor Text   *Brent turned toward his clock. It was five thirty-five. He hated the hours before a party. A nervous energy whipped back and forth inside him. He focused again on the computer's screen and careened through the video game's dark passages, firing at everything speeding toward him, borne along by the never-ending music.*
    "Brent!"
    His mother's voice echoed up the stairs. Brent paused the game. The firing and explosions ceased as if a window had been closed on a war.
    "Dinner!"
    "All right."
    He played on, chewing up the minutes that stretched before seven o'clock. Why couldn't you fast forward through time the way you could with a video? He flicked another glance at the clock. Five forty-one. Real-time was a drag.
    He went downstairs. His parents had started eating. When they'd moved to Chicago a few months before, they'd suddenly begun dining in the kitchen, where they'd put a small TV. Brent served himself from the counter, then took his stool at the island and watched with his parents.
    The Friday sports news was on, annotated by his father's grunts and snorts. Brent had learned to judge his moods from these. (pp. 3–4)
    —Paul Fleischman, *Whirligig*

LESSON

Apostrophe-thon

After looking at how the apostrophe is used on the chart, and then looking for it in their own writing, my students also need to see the apostrophe's use in a larger piece of professional writing. Students work in groups of three with pages 3 to 7 of Paul Fleischman's *Whirligig*. First, I read aloud Chapter 1. Then, I distribute the photocopied pages. I say, "We're going to go hunting for words that show possession or contraction." We discuss how we can look for any words that use apostrophes. Each group finds and highlights all the words that use apostrophes on these five pages, plus the possessive pronouns that are apostrophe-less. Once they have found them all, groups will categorize them in a chart like the one in the visual scaffold. I model reading through the first sentence: *Brent turned toward his clock.* "Is there a possessive in this sentence?"

"There aren't any apostrophes, sir."

"Right, but do any of the words show ownership?"

"*His.*"

I ask the kids to help me categorize *his* and record the object of its ownership while recording their answers on an overhead. Then I show them how to find a contraction and what to do with that. (Note: *O'clock* is a contraction that stands for *of the clock.*)

Of course, I meander around the room, listening in, asking guiding questions, correcting misconceptions, collecting information for the later debriefing of the activity. Kids get excited when they see the double possessives like *His mother's voice.* When the first group spots that, I walk them through it, then have them share how to fill it out on the chart, putting *his mother's* under possessive and then *voice* under the object of possession. If anything is off track with more than one group, I stop and reinstruct, checking the first few. Rich discussion about contractions and possessives and the apostrophe occur during this contextualized experience of pulling out the apostrophes from a real text, categorizing them, and ultimately internalizing the patterns.

Visual Scaffold

Apostrophe-thon

I model how to fill out this chart by categorizing the first few possessives or contractions used in the text, whether or not they have apostrophes. In groups, students complete the chart.

Apostrophe-thon			
Possessives (Ownership)		**Contractions (Squished words)**	
Possessive	Object of Possessive	Contraction	Words Unsquished
his *computer's*	*clock* *screen*	*they'd*	*they had*

Apostrophe Wall Chart

In each class, students share their own examples. Later, I combine them into one wall chart, with each quadrant "showing" the patterns of possessives and contractions with models. Note: Some indefinite pronouns like *everybody* and *someone* (In fact, all the *-bodies* and *-ones*) don't follow the possessive apostrophe pattern noted in the chart. These exceptions do take an apostrophe and an *s* in the possessive form.

Possessives	Contractions
Simmy's house	The apostrophe acts as a **squish mark** to show where letters were pushed out.
principal's crash	
Jordan's skateboard	
car's wheel	do not becomes don't
Askari's folder	I don't eat breakfast.
Jericha's book	doesn't haven't
Josh's necklace	didn't couldn't
Vanessa's pens	shouldn't can't
clock's hands	won't wouldn't
Arianna's bike	isn't

Pronouns ~squish~

Possessive Pronouns **NEVER** use an apostrophe	**She's** smart. **He's** intelligent. **We'll** succeed. (we will)
his necklace	
her brush	they're = they are
my behavior	she's = she is
their grades	it's = it is

The Verb:
Are We All in Agreement?

The verb is the heartthrob of the sentence. Without a verb, a group of words can never hope to be anything more than a fragment, a hopelessly incomplete sentence, a eunuch or dummy of a grammatical expression.

Karen Elizabeth Gordon, *The Deluxe Intransitive Vampire*

The verb is the business end of the sentence, the sentence's reason for being. That's where the action is. Without a verb, even if it's only suggested, there's nothing going on, just a lot of nouns standing around with their hands in their pockets.

Patricia O'Conner, *Woe Is I*

Use active verbs unless there is no comfortable way to get around using a passive verb. The difference between an active-verb style and a passive-verb style—in clarity and vigor—is the difference between life and death for a writer.

William Zinsser, *On Writing Well*

Verbs give writing energy.

Vicki Spandel, *Creating Writers*

One who never uses the visual power of verbs resigns himself to sentences that plod.

William L. Rivers, *Writing: Craft and Art*

117

4.1 Subject–Verb Agreement

OPERATOR'S MANUAL

In Plain English　　A verb expresses action, existence (state of being), or an occurrence. A subject is a noun or noun phrase that is *doing* or *being* something in a sentence. Verbs must agree with their subjects in number and person. According to Strunk and White (2000), "The number of the subject determines the number of the verb" (p. 9).

AKA　　Agreeing in number and person, singular and plural.

"First-person singular" or "third-person plural"—those words alone would suck the air out of any classroom. Would you want to keep listening? At the same time, Laurie Rozakis (2003) reminds us, "Agreement is a biggie, because it occurs at least once in a sentence" (p. 111). That puts it in perspective, and the angle I take is craft.

Throughout writer's workshop, I've already talked to students about the effect of which narrator they choose, first, second, or third person point of view. These lessons give us another chance to play with switching narrators and the different rhetorical effects each choice has, while at the same time we focus on verbs and their agreement with each subject type. So, part of crafting effective sentences is matching verbs to their subjects. Remember, much of this can best be taught in the context of correcting the errors as they occur, rather than trying to memorize all of this fairly complex information.

Note: If there weren't exceptions, it wouldn't be English. See the charts in the Appendix for exceptions with *be, do,* and *have* verbs as well as other top-billed irregular verbs.

Student Error　　*She don't even know me, but she haves this idea that I think I'm better then her.*

Behind the Error　　Desiree has a system: She uses *don't* and *have* with singular and plural subjects (the only time she shouldn't), and she is not alone in this. This is a common error found as a marker in many dialects.

Mentor Text　　*He **said** nothing in defense of himself. How **could** he? Everything his aunt **said was** true. He **was** ridiculously small. His ears **were** obscenely large. He **had been born** with his eyes open. And he **was** sickly. He **coughed** and **sneezed** so often that he **carried** a handkerchief in one paw at all times. He **ran** temperatures. He **fainted** at loud noises. Most alarming of all, he **showed** no interest in the things a mouse **should show** interest in. (p. 17)*
—Kate DiCamillo, *The Tale of Despereaux*

This paragraph brings up many points for discussion. We see immediately with the first verb that it isn't always as easy as adding an *-ed* to form the past tense. This passage could easily be a springboard into a discussion on irregular verbs.

From Past to Present—It's About Time . . . and Effect

First I read the passage from *The Tale of Despereaux* as an example of a text written in the past tense. "What tense is this in, past or present?" We may need to define or redefine terms, but out of the discussion we highlight (literally) the verbs and discuss what they tell us about time. For craft purposes, to get a sense of the different effects of past and present tense, we take the passage from *The Tale of Despereaux* and change it from past to present on the overhead.

We have already hunted down the verbs, so giving the passage a present-tense makeover is just a matter of taking "already happened" to "right now." We even get to dance around perfect tenses—we don't have to focus on that label, just on the concept that Despereaux had been born with his eyes open. When the passage is in the past tense, this event happened even farther in the past, or in the past "squared." When we shift the passage to the present tense, all we need is past tense to express that he was born before this paragraph occurs in time.

Next I show the students a paragraph I wrote in the present tense to see whether they notice the pattern:

> *With my bicycle secure in the roof rack high atop my Volvo, I drive home after my first 40-mile bike ride, and I feel so happy. So happy, in fact, without even thinking or slowing down, I drive into my driveway and into the carport. That is, until I hear a loud, horrible scraping sound. I slam on my brakes and watch in my rearview mirror as my $2300 Lance Armstrong Trek crashes down on my trunk, dragging its metal toe clips across the gold paint, finally dropping off the edge of the trunk, and dropping one final time onto the driveway. My high is officially over.*

I ask students what they notice about the verbs. Then I ask students to do a freewrite. It could be about a time they felt stupid or had an accident or a time they were feeling good after they did something for the first time. The only requirement is that they write it in the first-person point of view, and write in the present tense.

Next, we look at this same piece rewritten from a new point of view or perspective. I change the narrator from *I* to *he/she/it* (third-person singular):

> *With his bicycle secure in the roof rack high atop his Volvo, Thomas Segura drives home after his first 40-mile bike ride, and he feels so happy. So happy, in fact, without even thinking or slowing down, he drives into his driveway and into the carport. That is, until he hears a loud, horrible scraping sound. Thomas slams on his brakes and watches in his rearview mirror as his $2300 Lance Armstrong Trek crashes down on the trunk, dragging its metal toe clips across the gold paint, finally dropping off the edge of the trunk, and dropping one final time onto the driveway. His high is officially over.*

Again we discuss what we notice about the verbs. "How are they different?" I ask. Then, I ask everyone to rewrite their passages in the third person. We discover the patterns, singular and plural, the different effects, the different options we have as writers.

Visual Scaffold   **Subject-Verb Agreement Chart**

This visual scaffold is pre-made by the teacher so that students can generalize rules from the matrix. I use it to ask questions such as: What do you notice? Point of view? Which is the only voice or person in present tense that doesn't use the base verb? What about the past tense verbs? Are there exceptions? A reproducible version of this chart is provided in the Appendix.

Number	Subject		Verb	
	Point of view	*Present*	*Past* (Base + *ed*)	
Singular (one)	*I* voice (1st)	I walk.	I walk**ed**.	
	You voice (2nd)	You walk.	You walk**ed**.	
	He/She/It voice (3rd)	He walks. (Base + *s* or *es*)	She walk**ed**.	
Plural (more than one)	*We* voice (1st)	We walk.	We walk**ed**.	
	You voice (2nd)	You walk.	You walk**ed**.	
	They voice (3rd)	They walk.	They walk**ed**.	

Present and Past Tense Subject-Verb Agreement

A reproducible list of subject-verb agreement examples is provided in the Appendix.

Present Tense	In the "right now" or present tense, we add **-s** or **-es** to verbs only when matching to a *he/she/it* voice (third-person singular). Of course, any nouns that can be replaced by *he, she,* or *it* follow the -s rule.	He jump**s** for joy. (The subject match**es** the verb.) Richard jump**s** for joy.
	All other "right now" or present tense verbs are left as they are, the base verb.	I jump. We jump. You jump. They jump.
Past Tense	When dealing with things that have already happened or past tense verbs, we simply **add an -ed ending** to the base verb in all cases.	I/We jump**ed.** You jump**ed.** She/He jump**ed.** Veronica jump**ed.** They jump**ed.** Veronica and Al jump**ed.**

Dropped Inflectional Endings

OPERATOR'S MANUAL

In Plain English　Inflectional endings such as *-s, -es, -ed,* and *-ing* that are often dropped in speech and writing. Dropping an inflectional ending essentially drops the verb tense. This error is a close cousin to subject-verb disagreement, but it is strictly about articulating and attending to the endings of verbs.

AKA　Subject-verb disagreement, tense shifts, irregular verbs.

Often students come from a community where many inflectional endings are dropped in speech and writing. For example, they might say, "I use to drop verb endings" instead of "I use**d** to drop verb endings." In writing, those one or two letters at the end of a verb mean everything about when events happen. Readers cling to those kinds of clues, and when there is a shift, it better be necessary, by golly.

　　There is a link between wrong or missing inflectional endings and wrong tense or verb form, because without the *-s* or *-ed* endings, we aren't cued to the correct tense.

Student Error　*Anyways, Mr. Anderson ask Elvia, "Where you get them blue contact lenses, Elvia?" Then he got all mad when she say the flea market. So I knew better than to tell him they were mine.*

Behind the Error　Janie doesn't say the endings of words in the past tense either, so she won't be able to identify this error in her own writing. It is common for English language learners and other students to drop inflected endings like the *-ed* in *asked.*

Mentor Text　Any lead, the first two or three sentences, from any written work can be used.

I hate my life. I hate my father. I hate being fat. (p. 1)
—Paula Danzinger, *The Cat Ate My Gymsuit*

LESSON

The Verbs—They Are A-Changin'

To kick off this session on verbs and subject-verb agreement, I start with something simple. To merge craft with grammar, I look at leads (the first two to three sentences of a novel or a chapter, though nonfiction works as well). Let the masters of writing do the teaching.

　　Before the lesson, students take the first three lines of whatever book they are reading and record these lines as accurately as possible. (If you prefer, choose the first lines and distribute them to kids.)

　　For instance, look at the following example that Randy and his table discovered. When we looked at the lead from *The Dead Season* by Franklin W. Dixon (1990), we realized we shouldn't mess with the dialogue within quotes. They are words people said, after all, and the only thing that should change are the attributions or verbs, not what's between quotation marks:

"But you're the fourth cab driver we've asked," Callie Shaw **said** *in desperation. "Why won't anyone take us to Runner's Harbor?"*

> *"I don't know about anybody, but I'm on my break,"* **mumbled** *the cabbie.* (p. 1)

Randy's group liked how it sounded when changed to the present tense. They had to use that pesky *he/she/it* voice.

> *"But you're the fourth cab driver we've asked,"* Callie Shaw **says** *in desperation. "Why won't anyone take us to Runner's Harbor?"*
> *"I don't know about anybody, but I'm on my break,"* **mumbles** *the cabbie.*

Another student, Joshua, noticed he had to delete a *to* and move some words around when he changed the tense of his lead. The original, from Alvin Schwartz's *Scary Stories to Tell in the Dark* was *Pioneers used to entertain themselves by telling scary stories* (1981, p. 1). Joshua's version read: *Pioneers use scary stories to entertain themselves.* As Joshua said, "I wanted it to make sense, so I had to change it." It's that kind of meaning-restricted thinking I want my students to do with grammar and mechanics.

I tell students that writers don't want their leads to confuse readers. "We are going to see what we can learn from the writing mentors we have all over this room: The authors of the books we love." I put the lead from Paula Danzinger's book, *The Cat Ate My Gymsuit,* on the board: *I hate my life. I hate my father. I hate being fat.* "What tense is this in? Present? How'd you know?" I ask. I start filling in the verb tenses chart (see finished chart in the visual scaffold). "So, Danzinger left the verbs 'as is' to show the story was in the present." I write *leave verbs as is* on the present-tense side. I ask how we would put her lead in the past. As a student makes an oral change, I write the new sentences on the board: *I hated my life. I hated my father. I hated being fat.* We discuss how we made them past tense, adding this to the chart as well.

"What if I rewrote it from the third-person point of view, or the *he/she/it* voice? *She _____ her father.* How would you say this sentence? How did you know to use *hates?*" We discuss the "right now" present tense, and how the *he/she/it* voice messes it up by changing the pattern. We must add an *-s* or sometimes an *-es* with the *he/she/it* voice. We add this observation to the chart. Next we change the third-person lead to past tense. Students are so relieved to see that the *-ed* ending is consistent. (Wait till they discover the irregulars!)

Finally, I ask students to do the following:

- Find a lead and identify the verbs in the lead by underlining them. I encourage students to ask classmates at their tables for help and to raise their hands if no one can figure it out.
- Identify the tense (present, past, or something else).
- Form a group with those at their tables, and pick one lead as a group.
- Copy the original lead on a transparency and write to the side if it's in past or present tense or something else. Then beneath that, rewrite the paragraph, changing the tense, so changing the verbs only.
- Come to the front as a group, display the transparency, and work through it together, correcting it, discussing the differences, and adding any useful information to the chart.

Visual Scaffold   **Verb Tenses Chart**

I always have to make an additional poster to fit all the irregular verbs they come across. They love being able to find so many. Finding them while making the Verb Tenses wall chart creates numerous teachable moments that seem more like discovery than drudgery.

Verb Tenses	
Present—"Right now"	**Past—"Already happened"**
Leave verbs as is unless using the *he/she/it* voice.	Add *-ed* endings
He/she/it voice and all that would replace it, such as Patrick/Sarah/computer	Add *-ed* to all regular verbs, really!
I hate school	I hated school
She hates school	She hated school.
is	was
are	were
sit	sat
see	saw
run	ran
hear	heard

4.3 *Do* and *Have* Agreement Errors

OPERATOR'S MANUAL

In Plain English   The verbs *do* and *have* are considered auxiliary verbs, meaning *do, does, did, have, has, had;* all need to be used with another verb unless answering a yes-or-no question. But like regular verbs, *do* and *have* must match their subjects (*he does* versus *he do*).

AKA   Auxiliary verb agreement errors.

Incorrectly using the forms of the verbs *do* and *have* is another dialect issue. The nonstandard use of *do* and *does* pervades many dialects: Creole in Louisiana, pidgin in Hawaii, and African American in some urban and rural areas of the United States. This dialect issue is one that often needs to be addressed to show the child about code-switching for academic English.

   The problem can be easily addressed by referring back to students' previous knowledge of the verb patterns we use with all regular verbs in the present tense. To illustrate, we use *do* in the present tense with the *I* and *you* voices. However, like all regular verbs, when we use the *he/she/it* voice, we switch our verb form to *does. He does. She does. It does.* As luck would have it, *have* follows that same pattern in singular forms. *I have. You have.* And it switches to *has* for the third-person singular voice: *he has, she has, it has.* See the charts in the visual scaffold and the Appendix for the patterns for the plural and negative forms of *have.*

Student Error   *My auntie told me she don't like me hanging out at Ingram Park Mall. She have a problem with all the kids and not so many adults around to supervise.*

Behind the Error   Lynette is following the system she knows, the system her *auntie,* as she says, may use with her at home. I see the power of Lynette's words. She is naming specific places, noting cause-effect relationships in explaining why her Auntie doesn't like her going to the mall. If Lynette can learn one system, she can learn the standard system as well.

Mentor Text   *No one in living memory **had** ever been thrown out of Traybridge Middle School, but Jake Semple **had** managed to accomplish that feat in three weeks flat. (p. 2)*
*Jake **hadn't** been any more than two years old when he found out how certain words affected other people. It **had** surprised him considerably, since his parents used those words at home all the time. . . . Nobody could ever tell Jake Semple that words **didn't have** power. (p. 7)*
*(H)e was stuck with a bunch of strangers who **didn't** get it that he wasn't going to do what he **didn't** want to do. (p. 7)*
—Stephanie S. Tolan, Surviving the Applewhites

*The convicts we have are the kind the other prisons **don't** want. (p. 1)*
—Gennifer Choldenko, Al Capone Does My Shirts

LESSON

You Can't *Have* It All—If He/She/It *Has* Anything to Say About It

"Patterns. Verbs have patterns. What does that mean to you?" I begin. My fingers are mentally crossed, as I'm hoping that kids have let some of the rules we have learned sink in. A lesson on the verb forms of *have* is a perfect way to review a pattern that works for all regular verbs.

I entertain answers about past and present, about plural being more than one and singular being one. If no one hits on how the *he/she/it* voice (third-person singular) is the pattern breaker, I walk over to the wall chart on regular verbs and start tapping that section.

"The good news is this pattern will help us with other words as well. Take the verb *have* for instance." I put a sentence from the Newberry Honor book *Surviving the Applewhites* on the overhead with the word *have* removed.

> *Nobody could ever tell Jake Semple that <u>words</u> didn't _____ power.*

"What would you put in the blank? *Has* or *have*?"
"*Have.*"
"See, you already knew *has* wouldn't work, but what if you were stuck and weren't sure? How could you be sure?" I pass out the *Have* Verbs chart. After telling the kids to read it, I ask, "What pattern do you see?" Kids see the pattern, and I have them prove how the pattern works for the *Surviving the Applewhites* sentence we just looked at. The class and I connect this back to regular verbs.

"Okay, here are two more sentences from *Surviving the Applewhites*," I say, showing them these two sentences with the *have* verbs removed:

> *No one in living memory _____ ever been thrown out of Traybridge Middle School, but Jake Semple _____ managed to accomplish that feat in three weeks flat.*

> *Jake _____ been any more than two years old when he found out how certain words affected other people. It _____ surprised him considerably, since his parents used those words at home all the time.*

"With your writing buddy, I want you to fill in the blanks and be ready to explain why this answer fits the pattern on the chart." We also review past and present, if we need to. I ask questions such as: "What clues does the writer give you about the past? How old was he? Is it a memory or is it the present? What tense are the other words in the sentence?" We use the chart and the sentences to discuss and practice orally, using *has*, *have*, and *had*.

Easy Does It—He/She/It Again

I put this book title on the overhead: *Al Capone _____ My Shirts*. Then, I ask kids for some possible words to finish this title. Kids love coming up with improbables. "*Eats*," "*smelled*," "*shot*," "*made*," and "*makes*," they offer. To narrow the focus, I let the students know the title is in the present tense.

"Which words would we have to get rid of or change?" After we change *smelled* to *smell*, *shot* to *shoot*, we return to solving the case. I tell them who Al Capone was; that he was in a jail called Alcatraz, surrounded by water; and that the name of the book is *Al Capone Does My Shirts*. "Why isn't it *Al Capone Do My Shirts*?" I ask. If I have already given the other lessons on verb patterns, my hope is that the kids will tell me the answer, using the pattern. Maybe they will even help me make the pattern, but I have an already-filled-out chart, just in case.

I try to get students to answer with the pattern in mind. I start making a chart. "So, Al Capone is the *he/she/it* voice. And *does* goes with the *he/she/it* voice. What goes with *I* and *you*?" The kids tell me *do*, and I fill in the *I* and *you* voice on the chart. Next, we look at a sentence from the book.

The convicts we have are the kind the other prisons _____ want.

"*Do* or *does*?" I ask.
"Wait, it's *don't*," Vanessa says.
"Aha! Let's add that to our chart as well. Thanks, M'lady."
We fill in the negative versions with *don't* and *doesn't*. And then we see how the past tense side again gives us a free ride by never changing: It's always *did* or *didn't*. Students love it when our language gives them a break. We tie this back to *have* and all regular verbs, then we do a buddy check of our work to make sure we are following the patterns on the chart.

Visual Scaffold

Have Verbs Chart

If students are struggling with these verbs, I can run off a copy for them to keep in their notebooks or writing folders. *Have* verbs follow the same patterns as regular verbs. Think of *has* as the *-s* form of *have*.

Point of View (Person)	Singular	Plural
I/we voice (1st)	I have/haven't	We have/haven't
You voice (2nd)	You have/haven't	You have/haven't
He/she/it voice (3rd)	**He has/hasn't** **She has/hasn't** **Jericha has/hasn't**	They have/haven't Boys have/haven't
Past Tense ("Already happened") Use **had/hadn't** in all cases.		

Do Verbs Chart

Use *do* with every present-tense form except the *he/she/it* voice, third-person singular. We do say *I do*, but we never say *she do*—we say *she does* as *he does* (think of *does* as the *-s* form of *do*). Notice the pattern: See how again it is the *he/she/it* voice that is the exception, just like most other verb patterns.

Point of View (Person)	Singular	Plural
I/we voice (1st)	I do/don't	We do/don't
You voice (2nd)	You do/don't	You do/don't
He/she/it voice (3rd)	**He does/doesn't** **She does/doesn't** **Elliot does/doesn't**	They do/don't Friends do/don't
Past Tense ("Already happened") Use **did/didn't** in all cases.		

4.4 Unnecessary Shift in Tense

OPERATOR'S MANUAL

In Plain English   Verbs tell when the action in writing takes place. Another close cousin to subject-verb disagreement, this error focuses on consistency of tense and what shifts mean.

AKA   Subject-verb disagreement, inconsistent tense.

Keep your tenses logical and consistent. Within a larger narrative, verbs must live in the same time zone. Don't arbitrarily bob and weave from past to present to future. Within sentences, several things may each be in separate time zones.
—Constance Hale, *Sin and Syntax*

Although many professional writers shift tenses in their writing, there is always some reasoning behind the shift—an effect, a flashback, some shift in time. Even one sentence can contain more than one tense: *I love what you said yesterday.* But sloppy shifts in tense can really disrupt the flow of writing. Though tense shifting may occur in professional writing, students must discover that writers don't just shift tense without reason. Tense shifts mean something, so writers had better know what effect they are creating. In general, shifting tense midstream is marked as incorrect in student writing. We also know that shift in tense is a testable skill on state writing assessments. It's pretty cut-and-dried on a test. Consistency is the key. But in writing, the writer has to follow the guide of what makes sense. Of course, sloppy shifts like *I went to the store and eat candy* are wrong. I communicate to students that, at least at the paragraph level, verbs should stay in the same tense.

Student Error   *On Saturday mornings, the first sound I hear is my little brother's video game music. I put my head under the pillow, but the boing-boing-swup-swup is too much. I might as well get up. I pulled off my sheet and I make some breakfast. What will it be? Cereal? Yes, I take the Cinnamon Toast Crunch off the shelf.*

Behind the Error   Sarah is experimenting with writing in the present tense. That is worthy of praise, as is all that is right with this scene, such as the onomatopoeia (*boing-boing-swup-swup*) of the video game. She needs to be cued to be consistent with tense and only shift when there is a reason, a real reason, not "because it sounds better."

Mentor Text   **"My Name" from *The House on Mango Street* with the Verbs**
In English my name means hope. *In Spanish it means* too many letters. *It means* sadness, *it means* waiting. *It is like the number nine. A muddy color. It is the Mexican records my father plays on Sunday mornings when he is shaving, songs like sobbing.* (p. 11)
—Sandra Cisneros, *The House on Mango Street*

LESSON

Who Took the Verbs Out?

I give students a passage from *The House on Mango Street* (1984) that has some words removed. I ask groups of three or four to figure out what kind of words are missing, and then to fill in the blank spots with words that make the passage make sense.

As I listen to the conversations, I may nudge groups along with questions, but I try not to answer questions. Students want to know whether they are right, "Should they (the verb tenses) all be the same?"

I just respond with questions. "What do you mean?"

"Like the verbs. Do you have to always use *is* or can you use *is* and *was*?"

"Can you? See what works."

After we read each passage, I ask them some questions about the choices groups made:

- Which verbs did they choose?
- Do they make sense?
- Which tense did they choose? Did they stick with it? Why? Why not? Does it sound right? Is it clear?

If a student wants to argue that verbs have to agree, in whatever words they use, I let them go for it, helping them out here and there. "So, we have to make the verbs agree?"

Then, without further ado, I let them in on a writer's secret: Writers take the time to make their verbs agree to make meaning clear. Certainly, within one paragraph we should make our verbs the same tense, past or present. Next, students take out whatever writing they've done recently and do an express-lane edit, checking for verb tense consistency. Over the next several days I make sure to call their attention to verb tense in literature, reinforcing their knowledge of the ever-important verb.

Verbs Still Making Students Tense?

This lesson centers around the following passage, from which I have removed most of the verbs:

> *Walking into my Math class, I _____ the girl of my dreams sitting in the last desk of the first row. Her brown hair, swept to the right, _____ down on her shoulders. She _____ a bag of Doritos. Nacho cheese, my favorite. Could it get any better, I _____ to myself. And then she _____ at me. She _____ to speak to me. Her lips, outlined in brown, _____, "What are you looking at?" And the sound of my dream deflating _____ in my ear.*

In preparation for the lesson, I list the past- and present-tense forms of the missing verbs on a sheet of paper. These are:

see	saw
cascades	cascaded
eats	ate
thinks	thought
look	looked
is going	was going
open	opened
hisses	hissed

I photocopy the list, cut it into separate pieces, and place them in an envelope. I repeat this process until I have enough envelopes for groups of three in my largest class, plus a few extra for the unexpected. (See the Appendix for reproducible versions of the passage and the list of missing verbs.)

Before showing the passage, I divide students into groups, give each group an envelope, and ask them to categorize the words. They make all sorts of categories, but that's the point—to pay attention to the words, their connections. We talk about their categories. Some put all the words ending in -*ed* in one pile, and all the words that end in -*s* in another pile. There is no limit. Usually someone identifies the words as verbs, maybe even past and present verbs. If no one notices, I ask, "Do you notice anything that all these words have in common?" If no lights go on after looking again, I ask, "Are they nouns?" At this point, someone will step forward and identify them as verbs.

Now students categorize the verbs into two columns, past and present. We check and discuss. I give them the passage and ask them to choose the verbs they want to put in the passage. "Do we use all the ones from one column?" someone will ask.

"What do you remember about that?" I respond.

We check and compare and read the passage aloud both ways. "Why do you like one or the other better?" I ask. "What effects do the different tenses have?" We even have an opportunity in sentence 3 to look at showing ongoing action. "It wouldn't work in this narrative order to say *She ate a bag of Doritos*. How would we know?" We talk about why a paragraph, or chunk of meaning, makes more sense and is easier for a reader to follow when all the main verbs agree in tense. Here's another opportunity to review the key parts of a sentence.

I close with a review of why we do, in fact, seek to remain consistent with our verbs. Afterward, we do an express-lane edit and again focus on verb tense in our readings.

Visual Scaffold   **Verb Sorting**
Students complete a word sort, considering tense.

Adjectives and Adverbs: The Modifier Within

If you consistently use modifiers in irritating, monotonous, singsong patterns, break the habit promptly, decisively, and completely.

Patricia O'Conner, *Words Fail Me*

The adjective, no doubt, is the most maligned part of speech, and for good reason. For every adjective that is improving a sentence, ten are being written to the detriment of the sentences they inhabit. . . . The careless writer drags them in to provide information that would have greater impact if it came directly from the noun.

Gary Provost, *Make Your Words Work*

Adverbs can be useful, but we need to spend them like money. Never let an adverb steal work that should go to a worthy verb.

Vicki Spandel, *Creating Writers*

Some adjectives are definitely ambiguous.

Theodore Bernstein, *The Careful Writer*

5.1 Adjective Strings

OPERATOR'S MANUAL

In Plain English   When students rely only on adjectives to add detail to their sentences rather than on specific nouns and vivid verbs, they often create adjective strings—groups of three or more adjectives.

AKA   Adjective pileup, listy adjectives.

Shifting the adjectives out of their normal order creates a focus.
—Harry Noden, *Image Grammar*

Strings of adjectives—we've all cursed them at some point or another. Sure, an adjective has the power to transform a sentence. But we can't just stack them up into what O'Conner (1999) calls "assembly-line writing," sticking three or more adjectives before every noun. We often beg writers to add adjectives to their sentences, usually sharing something like this story O'Conner recounts from her childhood.

> *Mrs. Trotter, my fourth-grade teacher in Des Moines, once wrote a sentence on the blackboard—"The family sat down to dinner"—and asked us to imagine the scene. Then she added a word—"The Hawaiian family sat down to dinner" and asked us to picture the scene again. Everything changed: the room the people were in, what they looked like, the clothes they wore, the food they ate.* (p. 72)

O'Conner goes on to say that, by adding one word, her teacher transformed the sentence. An adjective can do an admirable job, both limiting possibilities and expanding meaning, making the word *family* both smaller and larger. Sometimes asking for adjectives, more adjectives, backfires and students overload sentences as a quick and shallow way to add depth or detail. When we pile up adjectives on noun after noun, it clogs up the flow of our sentences, making our ideas seem overdone—a gurgling, chatty assault on our senses.

Student Error   *My mom's new, large, blue Ford Expedition rides high above the other miniature, small, compact cars around us on the crowded, busy highway.*

Behind the Error   Annie's first set of adjective strings (*new, large, blue Ford*) tends to make the sentence sound less sophisticated and more clunky. We can celebrate the intent here. Annie is trying to plump up her sentence with details. The idea of "less is more" isn't in her developmental curve yet, so she'll need some scaffolding on other ways to add details and use adjectives. The second clump of adjective strings (*miniature, small, compact*) is another issue. Annie is learning that the thesaurus can give her words that have a "wow" factor. Again, the subtleties elude her, so I have to give her some opportunities to reflect on the effects of adjective strings.

Mentor Text   *A drunk guy staggers into my field, **red-eyed and swearing.*** (p. 2)
—Tracy Mack, *Birdland*

*Senora Wong, **diminutive but not fragile,** ruled with an iron fist.* (p. 6)
—Nancy Osa, *Cuba 15*

*Her eyes opened, closed, opened again, **pale and opaque.** (p. 149)*
—Gary D. Schmidt, *Lizzie Bright and the Buckminster Boy*

*The sun came up, as it had every day since the end of May, **bright, hot, and unrelenting.** (p. 1)*
—Jim Murphy, *An American Plague*

*Besides the guard tower, there's water all around, **black and shiny like tar.** (p. 4)*
—Gennifer Choldenko, *Al Capone Does My Shirts*

*Words were exchanged, **brief and hushed.** (p. 114)*
—Khaled Hosseini, *The Kite Runner*

*Nausea began to spread through his stomach, **warm and oozy and evil.** (p. 5)*
*He was aware of the other players around him, **helmeted and grotesque,** creatures from an unknown world. (p. 2)*
—Robert Cormier, *The Chocolate War*

The Human Sentence—Adjectives Out of Order

First, I make a sentence with three adjectives in a row, such as *The mangy, filthy, stray mutt approached me.* I take large sheets of construction paper and write each word on a separate piece of paper. I also put a period, two commas, and the word *and* on separate pieces of construction paper. When the class enters, I give the first fourteen students one of the words on construction paper. I tell the person with the *and* sheet to keep his or her seat until later. I ask the thirteen students (all except *and*) to come up front and make themselves into a living, breathing sentence using the words and the punctuation they have. They mill around a bit and start placing themselves. Jordan notices that his is the only card that starts with a capital letter, "Hey, I'm the first word!" There is some more negotiating, a little arguing, and without fail, the kids order their sentence as: *The mangy, filthy, stray mutt approached me.*

"Does it make sense?" I ask. The kids nod. "So, we created a sentence here that is correct and makes sense. But I am here to tell you that using a bunch of adjectives in a row is so third grade." We discuss how as writers we have many options when crafting a sentence. "We don't have to put the adjectives all in a row. Can anyone see another way to do it? What if I offered you the word *and*?" We think, and someone supposes we could leave the *stray* in front of *mutt* and move the *filthy and mangy* behind *mutt: The stray mutt, mangy and filthy, approached me.*

We talk about how we need the commas. Then, we match this pattern back to the interrupting sentence pattern. Students point out and compare how it works like an appositive by renaming the preceding noun. I read aloud a sentence from Jim Murphy's Newbery Honor book, *An American Plague* (2003). First, I read the sentence with the adjectives moved back to the traditional place—before the noun. Then for comparison I read the sentence as it is published. I say, "Listen to these two sentences. *The bright, hot, and unrelenting sun came up, as it had every day since the end of May.*" Then I read the sentence as it was published: *The sun came up, as it had every day since the end of May, **bright, hot, and unrelenting.*** We discuss the effects of moving the adjectives around and how the string sounds.

After that, we look at a few mentor examples from *The Chocolate War* and *Birdland.* In our writer's notebooks we play with the mentor sentences, reverting the adjectives back in the traditional order, reading and listening to the cadence—the way it sounds. We keep on the lookout for more adjectives out of order to record on our interrupter and closer sentence pattern charts. Then, we find a short piece in our writer's notebooks or a longer piece and try to break up a well-intentioned adjective string and shift some adjectives out of order.

Visual Scaffold

Human Sentence

Students negotiate an order to the words, and then line up in order. Note: My colleagues, Georgia Edwards and Cindy Tyroff, were inspired by Noden's *Image Grammar* (1999) when they created this "moving" lesson.

5.2 Adjective Clauses

OPERATOR'S MANUAL

In Plain English   An adjective clause works like a multiword adjective. It describes whatever is to the left of it, usually a noun. Adjective clauses are usually introduced by relative pronouns such as *who, whose, whom, which, that,* and *where.*

AKA   Relative clauses.

Adjective clauses can be difficult.
—Connors and Lunsford, *The Everyday Writer*

Adjective clauses give writers a way to identify which person or thing we are writing about. To illustrate, if I have a picture of three of my students that I am showing a friend, to discuss them individually I might say, "The student **who has her tongue stuck out** is Stephanie. The girl **whose hair is jet black** is Bianca." These dandy little adjective clauses give defining information to the audience to help them distinguish one student from the other.

   Since adjective clauses begin with relative pronouns, it's prudent to know, in general, when to use each one.

   • *Which* refers to things and animals.
   • *Who, whose,* and *whom* refer to people (or beloved animals).
   • *That* usually refers to things.

(*The Chicago Manual of Style* goes on to say that *which* is only used in the second and third person.) As for when to use commas with adjective clauses, clarity is the game. Different sources give different advice. Always use commas with *which* phrases and never uses commas with *that* phrases—unless of course, you need a comma for clarity. William Zinsser (2001) says, "Anyone who tries to explain 'that' and 'which' in less than an hour is asking for trouble" (p. 118).

   Do students even need to know the difference between adjective clauses and appositives? I believe they need to know the many options they have for layering information or detail into sentences, and adjective clauses serve that purpose whether you can name them or not.

Student Error   *The lady that drives our bus is crazy.*

Behind the Error   Clarity is well on its way in Alex's sentence. Alex has the concept that he needs to identify which lady he's referring to. Without a lot of explanation, I help Alex to see how using *who* instead of *that* when referring to people has a logic (as well as respect) to it.

Mentor Text   *It's the kind of smile you give to a chicken **whose** head you're about to cut off.* (p. 4)
*She opened the door—and stared beyond the picket gate at Willis Hurd and his friends, **who** all broke into a sudden and uproarious laughter—all except Willis, **who** was smiling his chicken-killing smile.* (p. 26)
—Gary D. Schmidt, *Lizzie Bright and the Buckminster Boy*

He did that thing again, **<u>where</u> he pulled back his lips and showed his teeth**. . . . It's hard not to immediately fall in love with a dog **<u>who</u> has such a good sense of humor.** (p. 12)
—Kate DiCamillo, *Because of Winn-Dixie*

Dead animals were routinely tossed into this soup, **<u>where</u> everything decayed and sent up noxious bubbles to foul the air.** (p. 2)
No one knew **<u>that</u> a killer was already moving through the streets with them,** an invisible stalker **<u>that</u> would go house to house until it had touched everyone, rich or poor, in some terrible way.** (p. 9)
—Jim Murphy, *An American Plague*

Which One? An Adjective Clause Tells All

I remove the adjective clauses from the mentor sentences above and type them on an overhead transparency—a trick I learned from Killgallon (1998) and Christensen (1968). As we look at the sentences, I say, "These are sentences from award-winning books. But I have done an evil thing, I have left off a part of each sentence." I share that I have left off the sentence parts so that we can see their effects more easily. I show them the sentences, which now look like this:

> It's the kind of smile you give to a chicken.

> She opened the door—and stared beyond the picket gate at Willis Hurd and his friends.

> Dead animals were routinely tossed into this soup.

> No one knew.

I then show students each sentence, one at a time, with the missing part added back to the sentence in bold. Following this procedure for each one, I ask, "What do you notice?"

Silence.

Finally, a student takes a stab. "Well . . . you added stuff."

We discuss what the head word (first word) of each added clause is. I write the head word of the clause, such as *whose,* on a piece of butcher paper or the board. I'll add the title of the chart later. "What does this *whose* clause do?"

"It says more about what kind of smile?"

I guide the conversation around to description and show the next sentence with its adjective clause restored, discussing what we notice, identifying the head word of the clause, and adding it to the chart. We keep looking at examples and adding to the list, completing it, and defining what kinds of adjective clauses usually go with each head word.

Later, we delve into literature, searching out adjective clauses, deconstructing and reconstructing them to see their effects.

Visual Scaffold

Adjectives Versus Appositives

If I want to move beyond the simplified term *interrupter,* I may want to clarify the difference between an adjective clause and an appositive.

Adjective Clauses **Tell which one**	**Appositives** **Rename** the noun
Influenza is a disease **which looms on often-touched surfaces,** waiting to infect its victim.	Influenza, **a silent stalker,** looms on often-touched surfaces, waiting to infect its next victim.

5.3 Adverb Clauses

In Plain English   Adverb clauses tell why, how, when, and under what condition things are or were done. Adverb clauses begin with subordinating conjunctions such as *after, although, as, when, while, until, because, before, if,* and *since* (AAAWWUBBIS).

AKA   Adverbial clauses, subordinate clauses, AAAWWUBBIS, dependent clauses.

Short eye-catching title patterns can not only tease the interest of the reader, but also provide a unifying idea of the image of the work.
—Harry Noden, *Image Grammar*

Since adverb clauses aren't sentences by themselves, they can be used as openers, interrupters, or closers. Often these dependent clause-causing words (*after, although, as, while, when, until, because, before, instead, since*) create sentence fragments in student writing because students don't understand the dependence or subordination that is caused by the AAAWWUBBIS.

Because adverb clauses are so handy, students may use them to expand sentences, telling how, where, when, why, or under what condition. Another way to merge AAAWWUBBIS with craft is to use these adverb clauses to create titles such as *Because of Winn-Dixie.* Noden suggests using grammatical constructs as titles: prepositional phrases and adverbial phrases; so, I thought, why not adverb clauses? The class and I create a chart of songs, movies, TV shows that begin with an AAAWWUBBIS as a head (first) word. While we are at it, we can merge in the mechanics of titles: Capitalize all important words (always the first and last words); use quotation marks around songs, poems, short stories, articles, and TV series names; and italicize or underline book, magazine, and movie titles.

Student Error   *Since you won't call me anymore. I don't want to talk to you at school either. If you call me tonight. We'll see about tomorrow.*

Behind the Error   Jennifer has learned the effectiveness of using subordinate conjunctions to link ideas and show relationships. Now I have to help her see that an adverb clause on its own is not a sentence, but they could make great titles, such as "Since You Won't Call Me Anymore" and "If You Call Me Tonight."

Mentor Text   "As the World Turns" (TV soap opera)
While I Was Gone—Sue Miller
Because of Winn-Dixie—Kate DiCamillo
"If I Can't Have You"—Yvonne Elliman
"Since You've Been Gone"—Kelly Clarkson

We're in the Titles

To keep the ever-useful AAAWWUBBIS in my students' consiousness, I use them to create titles for their work. "We're going to make another collection guys. Remember AAAWWUBBIS?"

We discuss how an AAAWWUBBIS is a sentence part and look at the words on the wall chart. I help students by explaining that when you start a clause with an AAAWWUBBIS, you know you might need a comma. "That's because it's a sentence part, not a sentence." We quickly review the uses of these subordinating conjunctions, and then I tell them they can be used to create fun titles.

"If you're ever stuck on coming up with a title, another way to come up with one is to try to start it with an AAAWWUBBIS," I say. I share a few titles such as *Because of Winn-Dixie*.

Visual Scaffold   **AAAWWUBBIS as Titles**

Many grammatical constructions make good starts to great titles. Subordinating conjunctions (AAAWWUBBIS) are no exception.

AAAWWUBBIS as Titles	
After	"After the Gold Rush," "After the Rain," *After the Fall*, "After the Lovin'"
Although (Even though and though)	"Even Though It's Over," *Although the Day Is Not Mine to Give*
As	*As You Like It, As a Falling Star, As a Favor, As a Man Grows Older, As a Man Thinketh, As Always, As American as Apple Pie, As Any Fool Can See, As Good as It Gets, As the World Turns*
When (Whenever)	*When I Was Little, When in Rome,* "When a Man Loves a Woman," *When a Boy Falls in Love, When a Man Loves a Walnut and Other Misheard Lyrics*
While	*While I Was Gone,* "While the City Sleeps," "While I Live," *While America Sleeps, While We Were Young, While You Were Sleeping*
Until	"Until Then," "Until We Meet Again," *Until Day Breaks, Until December, Until Further Notice, Until It's Too Late, Until Proven Guilty*
Because	*Because of Winn-Dixie,* "Because of You," *Because I Love Him, Because of Her, Because of the Rain*
Before	*Before Sunrise,* "Before I Say Good-Bye," "Before the Teardrop Falls," "Before They Were Kings," *Before Barbed Wire, Before Disaster Strikes, Before I Forget, Before Night Falls, Before She Met Me, Before You Get Your Puppy*
If	*If Looks Could Kill; If Bombs Fall; If He Only Had a Brain; If I Could; If I Ever Get Back to Georgia, I'm Going to Nail My Feet to the Ground;* "If I Never Knew You"; "If I Were a Rich Man"; *If These Walls Could Talk;* "If I Can't Have You"
Since	"Since You've Been Gone," *Since You Asked, Since You Went Away, Since Yesterday, Since Vietnam, Since I Was 25,* "Since I Don't Have You"

5.4 Adverbs and Conjunctive Adverbs

In Plain English　Adverbs tell when, how, where and to what extent an action or verb is done. Conjunctive adverbs show addition, comparison, contrast, example, summary, and time sequence by linking sentences and paragraphs.

AKA　Adverbial conjunction, transition words.

Adverbs and conjunctive adverbs can add depth and coherence to texts. Oftentimes they act as transition words to help guide a reader through a writer's ideas, signaling a contrast or comparison, or supporting an idea. Adverbs often end in the letters *-ly*, but of course there are exceptions, such as *today* and *now*.

On the other hand, conjunctive adverbs serve as transitional words or phrases such as *however, of course, nevertheless*. For a full list of conjunctive adverbs, see the Appendix.

The question becomes, when do you set adverbs off with a comma? The answer is often, if the adverb is at the beginning of a sentence, but not always. The best rule of thumb is clarity and effect. These words do often act as "comma magnets" when in opening, interrupting, or closing positions in a sentence. (See the Appendix for a list of transition words or conjunctive adverbs as well as "Comma Magnets as Sentence Openers.)

Student Error　*Awkwardly I walked down the hall. They yelled out names. Not nice ones of course. However I kept walking and acted like I didn't hear them. Sad and alone I went to lunch.*

Behind the Error　Charles is trying to make his ideas stick together with transitions and descriptions. On first glance, it would be easy to miss all the sophistication and fluency because of the missing punctuation. His ideas progress in a meaningful way; he just needs some sophisticated punctuation to go with his sophisticated composing. I helped Charles play with placing commas and showed him how that affected how I read his sentences. Charles ended up with this revision: *Awkwardly, I walked down the hall. They yelled out names—not nice ones, of course. I kept walking, however, and acted like I didn't hear them. Sad and alone, I went to lunch.*

Mentor Text　*Garret was the king of the phony farts at Trace Middle School. His most famous trick was farting out the first line of the Pledge of Allegiance during homeroom.*
　　　***Ironically,** Garret's mother was the guidance counselor at Trace Middle School.* (p. 10)
—Carl Hiassen, *Hoot*

*Mayor Clarkson, **meanwhile,** faced problems.* (p. 36)
—Jim Murphy, *An American Plague*

*He groaned, **quietly.*** (p. 22)
—Gary D. Schmidt, *Lizzie Bright and the Buckminster Boy*

LESSON

Adverbs, Adverbs Everywhere—Strictly Speaking

I put this sentence on the overhead: *"Uh, yeah," Garrett said.* I ask for a volunteer to read it. After the sentence is read aloud, I ask what clues the reader had for how to read it. Then I add a word to the sentence: *"Uh, yeah," Garrett said sarcastically.* We read it again and talk about the changes the word *sarcastically* brought with it. We talk about how the word functions to tell us how Garrett said the other two words, helping us know how to read it. Then, I add one more detail to the sentence: *"Uh, yeah," Garrett said, sarcastically.*

I ask, "What did I change?"

"You put in a comma."

"What difference will that make in the reading of this sentence? What should my voice do when it reaches the comma?"

"Pause."

The sentence is reread with a pause, and we discuss the effect and the choices we need to make when we are writing. Everyone finds some dialogue in a piece they've been working with and tries to add an adverb or transition words (conjunctive adverbs) to help add depth or cohesiveness to their writing. It is also crucial that I help students connect these adverb patterns with the three sentence patterns, so students see that an adverb such as *finally* tagged on the beginning of a sentence is an opener, an adverb such as *meanwhile* between two commas is an interrupter, and one such as *sarcastically* tagged to the end of a sentence is a closer. The positioning affects how it's punctuated.

Visual Scaffold

Lone Adverbs as Sentence Parts
This visual scaffold shows students how an adverb is one more way to create sentences with openers, interrupters, or closers.

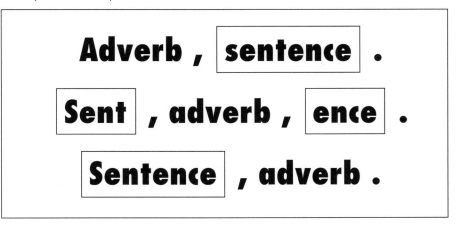

The Power of Punctuation: The Period Is Mightier Than the Semicolon

Don't overlook the power of punctuation. It's not just window dressing; it can change the meaning of a sentence 180 degrees.

Patricia O'Conner, *Woe Is I*

Punctuation in skilled hands is a remarkably subtle system of signals, signs, symbols, and winks that keep readers on the smoothest roads.

Rene Cappon, *The Associated Press Guide to Punctuation*

Punctuation herds words together, keeps others apart. Punctuation directs you how to read, in the way musical notation directs a musician how to play.

Lynne Truss, *Eats, Shoots & Leaves*

New conventions, such as word separation, features of layout and punctuation, were developed to make it easier for readers to extract the information conveyed in a written medium, and over the centuries these were gradually augmented and refined.

M. B. Parkes, *Pause and Effect*

However frenzied or disarrayed or complicated your thoughts might be, punctuation tempers them and sends signals to your reader about how to take them in. We rarely give these symbols a second glance: they're invisible servants in fairy tales—the ones who bring glasses of water and pillows.

Karen Elizabeth Gordon, *The New Well-Tempered Sentence*

143

6.1 Misuse of Quotation Marks

OPERATOR'S MANUAL

In Plain English   Quotation marks serve as visual clues to show readers when dialogue or quoted material is used in a written work. They may also clue readers to a quote within a quote or give readers information about a title.

AKA   Incorrect markers for dialogue, speech, titles, or quotations.

Quotation marks serve many functions. Writers:

- Use quotation marks around what is said aloud, signaling dialogue.
- Use quotation marks around direct quotations.
- Use single quotation marks ('quote', the apostrophe on the keyboard) when a quote is within a quote.
- Use quotation marks around the titles of short works (poems, short stories, songs, essays, chapter titles, article titles, TV and radio episodes).

Many claim that the quotation mark for dialogue started out to be a symbol of lips. Whether that's true or not, it's not a bad memory device for students to remember where to place those marks—whatever would be said aloud, while the lips are moving, goes between the quotes. Missing closing quotation marks are a common, often-tested error on state writing assessments.

From a craft perspective kids need to keep these things in mind when using dialogue in their writing. Does the dialogue move the story along, providing important information about the action or character development? If it doesn't, do you need it? It needs to sound like people talking, and the dialogue will benefit greatly when action is peppered into the exchanges. Action tags, as I will call them, help add a bit of information and keep dialogue from becoming singsongy. Last, but not least, *said* is not dead. Yes, we can and should use in *said*'s place lively verbs such as *snapped, muttered, chuckled, repeated, mouthed, snickered, breathed, sneered, bellowed, grumbled, insisted, whispered, roared, hissed,* and so forth. These specific verbs do add information and context to dialogue, but, the writer chirped, sometimes *said* is sublime. *Said* is definitely not dead.

Student Error   *"Hi," I said.*
"Hi," said Romero.
"What's up? I asked.
"Nothing. What's up with you? said Romero.

Behind the Error   Crystal is starting each quote on a new line, using attributions with her dialogue and, when she uses opening and closing quotation marks, she puts the end punctuation inside the quotation marks. She is actually doing a lot of things correctly here. On the mechanics surface, she needs to make sure she closes her quotes, a common error, and on a craft level, she needs help reflecting on what she is trying to accomplish with dialogue. Is it something we just put in, or do we need to make sure it is adding something significant to her piece?

Mentor Text   *"Loena, Violeta, could you find it in your hearts to join the rest of us?" she asked,* ***calling us by our Spanish-class names, hitting just the right note of sarcasm.***
(p. 6)
—Nancy Osa, Cuba 15

"Yes, Father," Hassan would mumble, ***looking down at his feet.*** *(p. 4)*
"You don't know what it means?" I said, ***grinning.*** *(p. 28)*
"What is it, Amir?" Baba said, ***reclining on the sofa and lacing his hands behind his head.*** *(p. 31)*
—Khaled Hosseini, The Kite Runner

Revealing Character—Tagging Dialogue with Action

Once my students and I have spent some time crafting dialogue and getting the basic conventions under our belts, I introduce the craft of making dialogue meaningful and correct. We first talk about the fact that dialogue should serve a function in our writing, telling us about character or moving the action along. We can edit our dialogue and not report everything that's said—exact wording is not necessary and often boring. We should be eavesdroppers to listen to the rhythm and flow of how people talk. This is also a great time to review a grammatical construction such as the participial phrase. We look at how dialogue is put together by professional writers. One thing many professional writers do is tag attributions with actions, and often writers use participial phrases.

On the overhead, I put a quote about a teacher from Nancy Osa's *Cuba 15.*

"Loena, Violeta, could you find it in your hearts to join the rest of us?" she asked, ***calling us by our Spanish-class names, hitting just the right note of sarcasm.***

"What does this tell you about the teacher?" I ask.
"She . . . she is their Spanish teacher." Sam says, squinting his eyes.
Ben adds, "And she is sarcastic. That reminds me of Mrs. ——."
"Great, Ben, you're doing what good readers do, making connections. And good writers, like Nancy Osa, tag information or action to the end of sentences to help break up dialogue, to reveal things about characters."

Next I put up a few quotes I have gathered from books that don't emphasize the conversation or story development of quotes as much as how writers weave in movement around quotes, such as these pulled from Hosseini's *The Kite Runner:*

"Yes, Father," Hassan would mumble, ***looking down at his feet.***

"You don't know what it means?" I said, ***grinning.***

"What is it, Amir?" Baba said, ***reclining on the sofa and lacing his hands behind his head.***

"What do you notice?" I ask. We discuss how we can *show* so much about characters by describing, or in this case, really narrating how they talk and move. Participial phrases, or *-ing* verbs, come to the rescue again, giving our writing detail as well as sophisticated sentence construction and comma usage. These constructions are concise and pack in a great amount of detail efficiently, zooming in on details, sharpening the image.

Then I have kids practice this technique in their own writing. This lesson also serves to integrate the sentence constructions I want them to use, putting them in front of their faces one more time.

Visual Scaffold

Revealing Character with Action Tags Wall Chart
Posting examples of what writers do gives students powerful strategies to improve their writing and sentence complexity. I encourage students to add to the collection.

Writers tag dialogue with action that reveals something about the characters.
"Yes, Father," Hassan would mumble, **looking down at his feet.** "You don't know what it means?" I said, **grinning.** —Khaled Hosseini, *The Kite Runner*

6.2 Overuse of the Exclamation Point

OPERATOR'S MANUAL

In Plain English   An exclamation point indicates extremes of anger or excitement. It can act like a visual scream or an emphatic command. This one mark can change the feeling of a word or sentence, giving a sentence an emotional context. Exclamation points also help onomatopoetic words make more of a *splash!* When the exclamation point is overused, however, its effectiveness is lost.

AKA   Overuse of exclamation mark.

Don't use it (an exclamation point) unless you must to achieve a certain effect. It has a gushy aura—the breathless excitement of a debutante commenting on an event that was only exciting to her: "Daddy says I've had too much champagne!" "But honestly, I could've danced all night!"
—William Zinsser, *On Writing Well*

In the family of punctuation, where the full stop is daddy and the comma is mummy and the semicolon quietly practices the piano with crossed hands, the exclamation mark is the big attention-deficit brother who gets over-excited and breaks things and laughs too loudly.
—Lynne Truss, *Eats, Shoots & Leaves*

In the tome *Pause and Effect* (1993), M. B. Parkes explains that punctuation encourages readers to interpret reading based on their experience. He uses this example: "Stop! Stop!! Stop!!!" (p. 1). Parkes suggests this "punctuation might be interpreted as an increase in decibels" (p. 2). Of course, Parkes isn't arguing for the use of multiple exclamation marks; he is trying to make the point that our punctuation choices have rhetorical effects beyond the look on the page.

As with everything, when we teach a mark of punctuation, students will use them with abandon. Over time we have to help students reflect on the exclamation point's rhetorical effects: how it sounds, how it looks, what it means, and how much is too much. When using emphatic punctuation like the dash and the exclamation point, students must consider that their overuse waters down their effect. It reminds me of maraschino cherries. My brother and I used to fight over the faded pink cherries in the canned fruit cocktail my mother served. One year, my mother gave us each a jar of maraschino cherries for Christmas. We ate them all in one sitting, and neither one of us has ever wanted another. When we had a few, they had a delicious effect, but when we ate and ate and ate them, they became disgusting.

Exclamation marks are like maraschino cherries: Too many make you sick.

When kids notice this, they also start to find other crafty ways authors achieve emphasis. Gary Provost advises, "Emphasis tends to flow to the end of a sentence, so if there is one word or phrase you want to say a little louder, put it at the end" (p. 32).

Student Error   *"Get off my side of the seat!!!!" I yelled. My brother was crossing the invisible line on the car seat between us. "No!!!!!!!! Stop!!!!!!!!!!! Mom, he's touching my side!!!!!!!*

Behind the Error   Luis knows that he wants to show intensity in his writing. As far as we can tell from his use of exclamation points, he was very upset—extremely so. The good news is he is using the exclamation point or varied punctuation to shape his message. Now, as a class, we reflect on how much is too much.

Mentor Text   *Across the top of the flyer writ in big letters were the words LIMITED ENGAGEMENT, then the letters said, "Direct from an S.R.O. engagement in New York City." Underneath that in big letters again it said, "HERMAN E. CALAWAY and the Dusky Devastators of the Depression!!!!!!"*

Those six exclamation points made it seem like this was the most important news anyone could think of, seems like you'd have to be really great to deserve all those exclamation points all stacked up in a row like that. (pp. 6–7)
—Christopher Paul Curtis, *Bud, Not Buddy*

LESSON

Exclamation Degradation—Reflecting on a Point's Overuse

I put the mentor text from *Bud, Not Buddy* on the overhead. After we read through it, we discuss the meaning of an exclamation point. "On what occasions do you use exclamation points?" I ask.

"When you're yelling."

"Yelling. How are you feeling when you are yelling? Are you a little mad or a lot mad?" We go on to discuss the extreme emotions that exclamation points are supposed to indicate.

"Do some things deserve more than one exclamation point?" I ask.

"Well, I guess you would use more than one if you were really, really, really yelling."

I put up an example, uncovering each command one at a time, asking "How would you say this one?" We respond chorally as a class.

> *Sit down.*
> *Sit down!*
> *Sit down!!*
> *Sit down!!!*

We discuss how each one was a bit different, but how, at some point, the extra exclamation points did no good. Maybe three in a row shows an increase in volume or upset, but more than likely they're too much of a good thing, like the maraschino cherries. They leave writing sticky sweet.

Then student groups take a photocopy of a few paragraphs of a novel or short story we've previously worked with and highlight all the exclamation points. They see that authors rarely use more than one in a row, and that in the scheme of things they aren't used that much, certainly not six times in a row. This experience hits home the idea that we can't just make our writing more exciting by inserting many exclamation points. We have to craft good writing, and save the rhetorical and emphatic power of the exclamation point by using it rarely and wisely.

Visual Scaffold   **Exclamation Point**
See the chart of punctuation's basic functions and the full punctuation guide in the Appendix.

!	**Exclamation Point**	**Indicates extreme pain, fear, astonishment, anger, disgust, or yelling**	**Don't overuse exclamation points! Really!! Cut it out!!!**

6.3 The Semicolon

OPERATOR'S MANUAL

In Plain English   A semicolon is a dot suspended over a comma-shaped mark (;). It separates two independent clauses or a list of items that already contain commas.

AKA   "Love child of the comma and period" (Rozakis 2003), "Supercomma" (Walsh 2000). Perhaps Walsh penned this name for the semicolon because it can join two sentences without a coordinating conjunction.

What the semicolon's anxious supporters fret about is the tendency of contemporary writers to use a dash instead of a semicolon and thus precipitate the end of the world.
—Lynne Truss, *Eats, Shoots & Leaves*

The semicolon is an ugly bastard, and thus I tend to avoid it. Its utility in patching together two closely related sentences is to be admired, but patches like that should be a make-do solution, to be used when nothing better comes to mind.
—Bill Walsh, *Lapsing Into a Comma*

It may seem as though a semicolon should be half of a colon, but that's not quite it. A semicolon can be used like a period. Say you have two sentences that you don't want to separate with the full stop of a period. You want to show a link between the two sentences. A semicolon can do the job on its own. Not like the snively comma that has to have a coordinating conjunction, one of the FANBOYS, to join two sentences. The semicolon can join two sentences flying solo. Can you tell I am a semicolon supporter? The semicolon also comes in handy when a list contains commas within each chunk of the list. The semicolon can help separate the phrases in the list without muddling with the commas.

Student Error   *Albert shouldn't have gone in the water, I told him not to.*

Behind the Error   This essay was filled with Angel's guilt over his brother Albert's near drowning. In an essay like this, I never feel it appropriate to correct a student's grammar. At the same time, it was an important piece for Angel and he wanted to take it to publication. It was easy to remind him of the option of using a semicolon to separate two sentences.

Mentor Text   *Dad did everything he could to be a good father. He showed interest in everything my brother and I did.* **We joined the Boy Scouts; Dad joined the Boy Scouts. We became junior volunteer fireman; Dad became a junior volunteer fireman.** (p. 126)
—David Rice, *Give the Pig a Chance and Other Stories*

Tonight, though, there seems to be a delay; I pick up from the chatter that something special is going on. (p. 23)
—Patricia McCormick, *Cut*

Ships came and went; men and women did their chores, talked, and sought relief from the heat and insects; the markets and shops hummed with activity; children played; and the city, state, and federal governments went about their business. (p. 9)
—Jim Murphy, *An American Plague*

LESSON

The Semicolon—The Lone Separator

I hand out a strip of paper to groups of two or three. On the strip of paper is one of the preceding mentor sentences. I ask each group to come up with an explanation for that interesting-looking mark they see that is neither a comma nor a period. Some even say the period is resting on top of a rising comma. To make their conversations easier, I let them in on the secret that it's a semicolon.

One group asks whether they can look in the dictionary. I say, "In a minute. For now just look at the sentences. You and your group write out what you think it does. What mark is it like? What mark is it not like? What does it do?"

I listen in on the small groups and watch them struggle to compose a definition: "This is hard," "Well, it's like a comma and like a period," "No because you don't need one of the FANBOYS (coordinating conjunctions)."

After each group shares, we look at the sentences together and decide that the semicolon is most like the period. Students say it's least like the exclamation point because there is not excitement—just connection. I read them aloud what Strunk and White say about the semicolon, and then we dive into some recent writing. We find two or more sentences that are connected, and we play with semicolons.

Visual Scaffold

The Semicolon Explanation
See the chart of punctuation's basic functions and the full punctuation guide in the Appendix.

; Semicolon	Links independent clauses with similar ideas. May be needed when there are already too many commas in a sentence.	Between the period and the comma lies the semicolon. When items in a series contain commas, use a semicolon for clarity.

6.4 The Colon

In Plain English   A colon consists of two dots, one above the other. The colon is like a drum roll announcing what will follow. A complete sentence may end with a colon if there is a summary, idea, or list that follows.

AKA   "Punctuation's Master of Ceremonies" (O'Conner 1996).

Like a well-trained musician's assistant, it (the colon) pauses slightly to give you time to get a bit worried, and then efficiently whisks away the cloth and reveals the trick complete.
—Lynne Truss, *Eats, Shoots & Leaves*

The colon sets readers up to anticipate what follows, so it better not let the reader down. Most of the time a complete sentence leads up to the colon, which is a dot suspended over a dot (:). The colon may be followed by a list, another sentence, or a summary. Generally, the colon doesn't follow a verb. If what follows the colon is a complete sentence, it is often capitalized, but not always.

Student Error   *Then there I was: the bad son who didn't watch after his little brother.*

Behind the Error   Hold your breath. I didn't correct the verb preceding the colon because Angel really got the concept of the colon. I knew I could teach him that without stamping down his experimentation, which was triumphant for a closing line of a heartfelt essay. I also know that, like fragments, writers do it. As much as I wanted to write a revision such as this one, I didn't: *There I was, sitting on the dock: the bad son who didn't watch his brother.*

Mentor Text   *She took everything in then, and I with her:* **the house with the sloping roof, the evergreens leaning over it, the dark shadow that was the woodpile on the front porch.** (p. 91)
—Patricia Reilly Giff, *Pictures of Hollis Woods*

The morning the Reeds' baby died was June 5: **a day shimmering with light, the smell of lilacs hanging sweetly in the willow tree behind the house where Alyssa was hiding.** (p. 1)
—Susan Shreve, *Blister*

LESSON

The Colon—The Drum Roll of Punctuation

I open with a sentence from *Pictures of Hollis Woods*. "What do you notice about the punctuation?" We discuss the commas after each item in the series and how there isn't an *and*. After pondering that for a bit, we turn our attention to the colon. "What is this mark doing?" I ask.

"It's like saying here's a list," says Alison.

"Okay, it's like get ready because here it comes," Richard adds.

"Exactly. I think of it like a drum roll," I say. I reread the sentence with a dramatic pause. Next I show them a colon in a lead from *Blister*:

The morning the Reeds' baby died was June 5: **a day shimmering with light, the smell of lilacs hanging sweetly in the willow tree behind the house where Alyssa was hiding.**

I show students another lead to part one of a book I am reading, *The Devil in the White City* by Erik Larson (2003):

How easy it was to disappear:
A thousand trains a day entered or left Chicago. (p. 11)

After we exhaust what the colon does, I play a clip from "Anticipation" by Carly Simon, telling the kids it's the colon's official theme song. "Really?" I tell them that the English teachers all over the world have a blog and we decided . . . Kidding. But they remember what the colon does.

Before we practice writing a lead with a colon, a sentence with one, or one that precedes a list, I give them the shorthand. We should try to make a whole sentence before the colon, and we'd better be announcing something interesting or surprising or listing something. For rules beyond that, we see what emerges. (Capitalize a sentence after a colon if it's a complete sentence, if you want. Never capitalize phrases or clauses that are not complete sentences.) The students help me write a few leads for my essay.

So many things ruined my eighth birthday: I asked for a present Dad didn't want me to have, I couldn't learn my multiplication tables, and my parents decided to get a divorce.

Today is my birthday: Nothing can ruin this day.

I put on the music again, and students rewrite a few leads, using the colon.

Visual Scaffold   **The Colon Explanation**
See the chart of punctuation's basic functions and the full punctuation guide in the Appendix.

	Colon	Announces a surprise or a list. Acts as a drum roll for something to follow.	Capitalize the first word after a colon only if it's a proper noun or the start of a complete sentence.

6.5 The Dash

OPERATOR'S MANUAL

In Plain English　A dash is used to set off information in a sentence with a dramatic flair. It may set off parenthetical information or a list.

AKA　Em dash, interrupter.

The dash has been frowned on by grammarians—if you are writing for a grammarian, don't use it—but I find it is a wonderful device to use to interrupt your line or comment on what you have just written, to give information the reader needs at the moment, to qualify or emphasize.
—Donald Murray, *The Craft of Revision*

Advice about using the dash always comes with a caveat, such as: "[an] invaluable tool . . . widely regarded as not proper—a bumpkin at the genteel dinner table of good English" (Zinsser 2001, p. 116) or "in abundance they suggest . . . hyperactive silliness" (Truss 2004, p. 158). On the other hand, the dash is also proposed as a perfect tool to show interruption in speech—or to dramatically set off extra information or a list in a sentence—dramatically. Like the colon, the dash calls attention to what follows it, telling our eyes to rush to the words after it. In fact, the word *dash* has its roots in the verb *dash*. The mark literally hurls us toward what follows. But keep in mind two principles: Use the dash sparingly and use it dramatically.

　　Although the dash can be used like a comma or parenthesis to set off parenthetical information, "the dash is strong punctuation that demands strength of the words it isolates" (Rivers 1975, p. 184). So we need to make sure our set-off phrase or list is significant or deserving of the power of the dash. When typing, create the dash with two hyphen marks to distinguish it from the hyphen.

　　Let's be honest. It's hard to misuse a dash. Unless you are setting off something that doesn't deserve a dramatic disjunction, it's hard to mess up. My students rarely, if ever, use the dash. Like other writer's options, students need to look at the dash in effective texts, to experiment and play with it.

　　To sum up, the dash can be used to show breaks in thought, appositives, summaries, lists, interrupters, closers, and even attributions, but, and this is a big *but*, we shouldn't overload our writing with them just because we can. (For more on the dash, see the punctuation chart and punctuation guide in the Appendix.)

Student Error　*Mom told me to stop, I wouldn't ever, but she didn't have to know that.*

Behind the Error　Elsa's only real error is that she has a comma splice or a run-on sentence. This is not a true dash error, like using a hyphen as a dash or vice versa. Yet, a dash could serve her in this instance. Elsa wants her sentence to keep a quick pace, which is why she uses a comma rather than a period. A dash enclosing "I wouldn't ever" achieves an emphasis that matches the rest of Elsa's essay on her defiance of her mother's rules: *Mom told me to stop—I wouldn't ever—but she didn't have to know that.*

Mentor Text　*DARKNESS—COLD—CHURNING WATER—roaring, like a thousand lions—spinning around and around—bashing into rocks—arms wrapped around my face to protect it—tucking up my legs to make myself smaller, less on target.*
　　Wash up against a clump of roots—grab hold—the wet roots feel like dead fingers clutching at me—a space between the water and the roof of the tunnel—I draw

quick gasps of breath—current takes hold again—trying to fight it—roots break off in my hands—swept away. (p. 5)
—Darren Shan, *Cirque Du Freak #6: The Vampire Prince*

Nothing ever seems interesting when it belongs to you—only when it doesn't. (p. 7)
—Natalie Babbit, *Tuck Everlasting*

Dashing—Simply Dashing!

I like to start off with these first two paragraphs from the much-loved series *Cirque Du Freak* for a few reasons. First, the dash—in some minds—is overused. But the main reason I use it is for the effect of the dashes on the text itself and its reading. The racing, moving text helps "show" in a quick way all the dash can do, and it sets up a furtive discussion on what works with the dash and how much is too much.

I read it aloud and then pass out a copy of the *Cirque Du Freak* mentor text. After students read it again silently, I ask, "What do the dashes do in the writing?" We discuss the effects the dashes have, making us almost breathless, breaking up thoughts, slamming the reader around like the narrator rushing through the water. I explain that the dash comes from the same root as the verb *dash*. Some students connect it to the character, Dash, in *The Incredibles* movie.

Referring back to the mentor text, I ask, "Do you think Darren Shan continues the whole book this way?"

"No. Because you'd never catch your breath. It's exciting for a while but you have to have, like, more stillness sometimes, so you can feel the rushing," Sam offers.

"So, too much of a good thing makes the good thing not so good anymore. It loses its effect."

When students can observe a principle or rule, they internalize so much more than they do when we just tell them. Next, I show them sentences with dashes from *Lizzie Bright and the Buckminster Boy*. As we look at each example, we discuss what we can learn about dashes from the author, Gary D. Schmidt, always making connections from the known to the new. "See the way the dash interrupter acts just like the interrupter you use with a comma?" We look at all the ways the dash fits into the patterns we know, reinforcing what we know and adding to our repertoire of rhetorical devices.

Visual Scaffold   **The Dash Explanation**
It is crucial that I continually make connections between all the sentence patterns, showing new ways we can use the same patterns. Students can see that they can use a dash much like a comma, but for different purposes and effects.

Lizzie Bright and the Buckminster Boy: Gary D. Schmidt Shows Us How to Use a Dash

Opener	*Rushing, rushing, rushing, waiting, waiting, waiting—swinging.* (p. 6)
Interrupter	*He began to paint, while the stars behind him glittered for all they were worth—**which was considerable**—and every single one of them held its place in the night's sky without falling.* (p. 144)
Closer	*He wouldn't go for the double—**just a single.*** (p. 5)
	*He looked at Turner, and Turner saw his eyes—**distrust.*** (p. 71)
List Pattern	*"More to the point," said the tallest of the group—**the one with the most expensive frock coat, the most expensive top hat, and the most expensive shiny shoes.*** (p. 19)
Compound Pattern	*Turner wondered if she might even fall asleep—**so** he played soft and low.* (p. 148)

Connect to the Three Complex-Sentence Patterns

Opener—sentence.

Sent—*interrupter*—ence.

Sentence—*closer.*

6.6 The Hyphen

In Plain English   A hyphen is a short horizontal line that joins adjectives or words to create one concept or unit.

AKA   Though often referred to as a dash, it's not. It's a hyphen.

The hyphen, a wee thing, is the shortest of the family.
—John Trimble, *Writing with Style*

That's right, the hyphen is shorter than the dash—the other member of the horizontal-line family of which Trimble speaks. On the keyboard, the dash is made with two hyphens as a matter of fact, making the hyphen half as long as the dash. The hyphen has its own purposes as well.

Primarily, the hyphen is used to connect words that the writer wants to show are related, to enhance and clarify description. Maybe we want to use a compound adjective; the hyphen is a well-suited solution. When I write *do-it-yourself scaffold*, I hyphenate the words *do it yourself* because as they came before the noun, *scaffold*, the words, as modifiers, needed to be joined to show that they operate together. Trimble (2000) suggests a test to see whether a multiple modifier needs to be hyphenated:

> *Hyphenate modifiers if you can't*
> 1. *reverse their order or*
> 2. *remove one of them without damaging the sense.* (p. 131)

Perhaps you want to join two or more words that make a concept like *six-pack* or *son-in-law* or *on-the-fly*. These hyphens show that these words are now operating as a unit. We also use the hyphen to join numbers *twenty-one* to *ninety-nine*. And the hyphen sets off prefixes in words such as re-sign (meaning to sign again, rather than to resign from a job). The hyphen helps break up words that could be confused without the break. After my first year of teaching, my principal called me into the office because I had checked off *intend to resign,* which to me meant to "re-sign" my contract for another year. Luckily, the problem was fixed before I showed up in September without a job. In *Eats, Shoots & Leaves,* Lynne Truss says it best, "A re-formed rock band is quite different from a reformed one" (p. 171).

Oftentimes, with common use, hyphenated words such as *e-mail* or *semi-colon* slowly make a shift and are no longer hyphenated (*email, semicolon*). *To-morrow* and *to-day* used to take a hyphen, but today you would think it strange. Put it this way: Time absorbs many hyphens. Before you think too long about the hyphen, ponder this statement from Truss, "In the end, hyphen usage is just a big bloody mess and likely to get messier" (p. 176).

Student Error   *I was a happy go lucky kid with not much on my never worry brain.*

Behind the Error   Jordan combines a cliché such as *happy-go-lucky* with a *never-worry-brain,* making it fresh again. Jordan has heard these concept adjectives in stories and on TV, and he is taking a risk by trying something new. He hasn't, however, seen the hyphenated words in print enough to insert hyphens when he writes.

Mentor Text   *D-day,*

*Or should I say **E-Day**, as in Envelope Day. Jilly and I stood on her front porch, fighting for the small amount of shade from the maple planted several feet from the house. The air was still and hot, and we fanned ourselves in quick bursts with the identical envelopes we clutched in our hands. In these envelopes were our futures. Molly Brown Middle School divided each **seventh-** and **eighth-grade** class into three "tracks" of about 150 kids. So rather than feeling like a small fish in a **450-student** pond, we'd feel like a small fish in a 150 kids.* (p. 3)
—Denise Vega, *Click Here*

*I heard the **click-clack-click** of dominoes and smelled the cigar smoke before I found Dad and Abuelo relaxing on the **screened-in** back porch.* (p. 22)
—Nancy Osa, *Cuba 15*

Hyphen Nation—Some Words Just Belong Together

We look at the paragraph from *Click Here* on the overhead. "What's a hyphen?" I ask. If I get no answers, I say, "Is there a punctuation mark you see in this paragraph that you don't know the name of?" We discuss what we know and that the little short minus sign is probably the hyphen. If you're lucky, you will have a student with a hyphenated name who will share with the class. As a class, we highlight all the hyphens we see in the passage.

"What are these hyphens doing?" I ask.

"Joining?"

"Joining what?" I smile.

"I don't know . . . words?"

"Yes, words, okay. What are the words doing to the noun after it?" I circle the nouns *class* and *pond*.

"Describing it," blurts out Krista.

We continue discussing function, how we join these words that come before a noun together. We talk about Trimble's test. We look at another sentence with hyphenated words that lets Nancy Osa show us how we do it.

*I heard the **click-clack-click** of dominoes and smelled the cigar smoke before I found Dad and Abuelo relaxing on the **screened-in** back porch.*

"How does Nancy Osa use hyphens?" We discuss how she uses them for onomatopoeia and to join two words describing the porch. For fun, I like to show the students a great picture book that uses hyphens in the extreme, describing heat. *How Hot Was It?* by Jane Barclay (2003) pours out phrases such as: "It was an icky, sticky, nerve-grating, tie-hating, wish-I'd-fixed-the-air, grouchy-as-a-bear kind of hot" (p. 10). Be careful. Hyphens like these are addictive.

Visual Scaffold   **Hyphen Explanation**
See the chart of punctuation's basic functions and the full punctuation guide in the Appendix.

██████	Hyphen	Indicates that two words should be thought of as one, especially when using two adjectives or groups of words that are acting as a unit.	**Writers use hyphens to** • join compound adjectives before a noun (*hard-working student*) • join compound nouns and two-word and multiple-word concepts (*mother-in-law, over-the-counter, twelve-year-old, know-how, skin-deep*) • most sources no longer recommend hyphenating paired nationalities (*African American, Italian American*) • add a prefix to a word when clarity is needed or to avoid doubling vowels (*anti-intellectual*) • divide lettered words (*T-shirt, L-shaped, X-ray, U-turn*) • divide a word between syllables at the end of a line: *When in doubt about hyphen-ation, check your dictionary.*

Appendix

Sentence Smack Down!

Group Directions

1. Identify the subject and the verb of your group's sentence first. Underline the subject and put explosion marks around the verb.
2. Assign roles:
   a. Reader: _____
   b. Subject: _____
   c. Verb: _____
3. Subjects write the subject of the sentence in large letters on a piece of construction paper. Verbs write the verb of the sentence in large letters on another piece of construction paper, surrounding it with exploding marks to connote action.
4. Then identify the subject and the verb for all the other sentences.

Examples

Then he lowers his hand.
Who or what does something? (He) What does he do? (lowers) He lowers.

His ears echo the thousand warnings of his mother: "Don't cross the street."
Who or what does something? (ears) What do the ears do? (echo). Ears echo.

Group 1:   You just cross paths now and then.
Group 2:   You don't even know his name.
Group 3:   At first Zinkoff shades his eyes.
Group 4:   He reaches back to touch the door.
Group 5:   Burping, growing, throwing, running—everything is a race.
Group 6:   Heedless of all but the wind in his ears, he runs.
Group 7:   Zinkoff gets in trouble his first day of school.
Group 8:   In fact, before he even gets to school he's in trouble.
Group 9:   The school is only three blocks away.
Group 10: Mrs. Zinkoff looks up the street.

Bonus Sentences

Their mothers holler at them for running in the streets, so they go to the alleys.

He squints in the sun, tries to out stare the sun, turns away thrilled and laughing.

Not a fence in sight.

He runs some more, turns right again, stops again.

Sentence Smack Down Performance

1. Reader reads group's whole sentence.
2. Subject smacks him- or herself on the wall mat under the Subject side, holding the construction paper subject at chest level and yelling the word.
3. Verb smacks him- or herself on the wall mat under the Verb side, holding the sign at chest level, yelling the verb.
4. Reader reads the sentence again.
5. Players exit as champions to music.
6. As other groups perform, check your answers.

Mechanically Inclined: Building Grammar, Usage, and Style into Writer's Workshop by Jeff Anderson. Copyright © 2005. Stenhouse Publishers. All rights reserved.

Mechanically Inclined: Building Grammar, Usage, and Style into Writer's Workshop by Jeff Anderson. Copyright © 2005. Stenhouse Publishers. All rights reserved.

List of Common Prepositions

Location		Time	Other Relationships
above	inside	**after**	about
across	into	**as**	despite
against	near	**before**	except
along	off	**during**	for
among	on	**since**	like
around	out	**until**	of
at	outside		per
behind	over		than
below	past		with
beside	through		without
between	to		
beyond	toward		
by	under		
down	underneath		
from	up		
in	within		

The Time words in bold may also function as *subordinate conjunctions*. Words can only serve one function per sentence. Tip: Prepositional phrases *never* have verbs.

Common Confusions with Spelling

Of, to, and *in* are among the ten most frequently used words in English—the most popular prepositions—so we have to get these right:

- I go **to** the dance. (Not too, which means also: *I danced a lot, too.* Not two, which means the number 2: *I did two slow dances.*)
- I ate a bag **of** candy. (Not off, which means away or indicates separation or distance between two points: *Therefore, I need to take off some weight.*)

Compound and Serial Comma Sentence Pattern Scaffolds

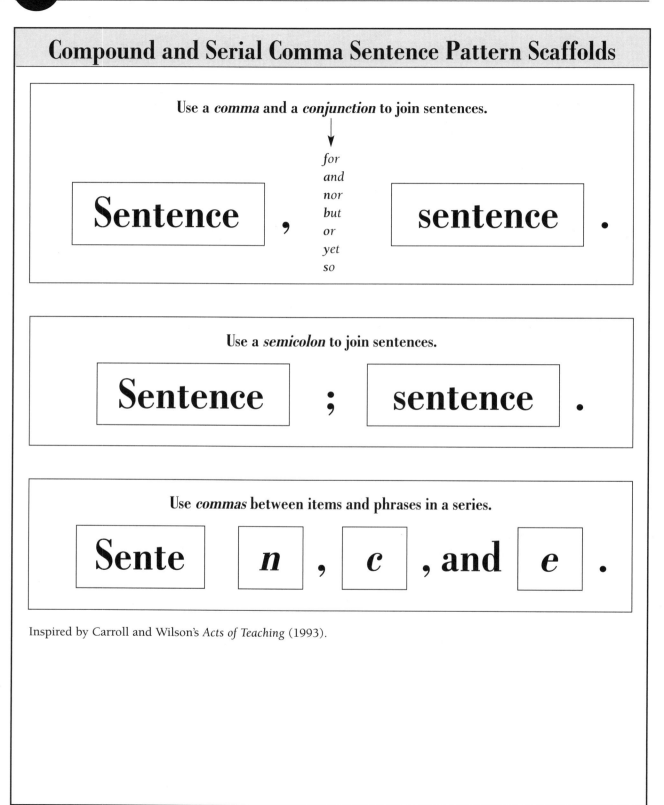

Use a *comma* and a *conjunction* to join sentences.

for
and
nor
but
or
yet
so

Sentence , sentence .

Use a *semicolon* to join sentences.

Sentence ; sentence .

Use *commas* between items and phrases in a series.

Sente n , c , and e .

Inspired by Carroll and Wilson's *Acts of Teaching* (1993).

Mechanically Inclined: Building Grammar, Usage, and Style into Writer's Workshop by Jeff Anderson. Copyright © 2005. Stenhouse Publishers. All rights reserved.

Mechanically Inclined: Building Grammar, Usage, and Style into Writer's Workshop by Jeff Anderson. Copyright © 2005. Stenhouse Publishers. All rights reserved.

AAAWWUBBIS and More!

Common Subordinating Conjunctions

After	After what seemed like forever, Royal finally slowed the team to a trot and then to a walk. —Jennifer Donnely, *A Northern Light,* p. 78
Al*though* (*Even though* and *though*)	Although Vincent is gone, I can still have fun without him. —Miguel Espinoza, sixth grader
As	As I walked outside for recess, he was almost certain there'd be a gold star next to his name when he returned. —Louis Sachar, *There's a Boy in the Girls' Bathroom,* p. 97
When (*Whenever*)	Whenever Ms. Franny has one of her fits, it reminds me of Winn-Dixie in a thunderstorm. —Kate DiCamillo, *Because of Winn-Dixie*
While	While he eats lunch, he talks about what he will eat for dinner. —David Klass, *You Don't Know Me,* p. 30
Until	Until then, Marian had never really thought much about vocal technique. —Russell Freedman, *The Voice That Challenged a Nation,* p. 14
Because	Because she is holding the microphone so close to her face, each moment of contact sounds like a heavy blow. —Myla Goldberg, *The Bee Season,* p. 276
Before	Before last summer, before the man ever came to town, I figure I was getting ready for him. —Cynthia Rylant, *A Fine White Dust,* p. 4
If	If you don't lie to anyone else in the world, you shouldn't lie to yourself either. —Gordan Korman, *No More Dead Dogs,* p. 28
Since	Since fourth grade, she'd kept a running list of them and liked to reread it to see if she could get the stories to go further in her head. —Naomi Shihab Nye, *Habibi,* p. 13

Subordinating Conjunctions by Functions: Dependent Clause Causers Revealed

Time	*Cause-Effect*	*Opposition*	*Condition*
After	As	Although	As long as
Before	Because	Even though	If
During	Since	Though	In order to
Since	So	While	Unless
Until		Whatever	Until
When/Whenever			Whatever
While			

Comma Magnets as Sentence Openers

Introductory words, such as adverbs, and transitional words that indicate order or time, are usually followed by a comma. Basically, you could be wrong if you left a comma off; however, you'd be fine if you put it in, whether you need it or not. Here are a few:

Addition Signals

In fact	In fact, most transitional words or phrases need commas after them when they open a sentence.
For example	For example, a long introduction always needs a comma after it.
In addition	In addition, the ear often signals a pause where a comma may be inserted after a transitional phrase.

Time Transitions

Next	Next, we should consider putting a comma after introductory time words.
Meanwhile	Meanwhile, we should also consider that the comma may not be needed.
Afterward	Afterward, you may just want to insert the comma anyway.

Contrasting Connectors

However	I like science; however, I don't want to become a scientist.
On the other hand	On the other hand, I enjoy history and I want to be a(n) historian.
Yet	Yet, I will never be a mathematician.

Adverbs or Adverbial Phrases

Basically	Basically, adverbs end in -*ly*.
Actually	Actually, you should know adverbs tell how, where, and when as well.
Eventually	Eventually, you'll know that adverbs add on to verbs to tell how, where, when, and what condition.
Of course	Of course, you don't put commas after every adverb.

Mild-Mannered Exclamations

Yes	Yes, yes is a mild exclamation.
No	"No, we still put the comma after *no* in dialogue," said Chris.
Well	Well, sentences shouldn't really begin with *well*, but when they do, *well* had better have a comma after it.

Note: Many of the words above often need commas on both sides when they interrupt in the middle of a sentence.

Mechanically Inclined: Building Grammar, Usage, and Style into Writer's Workshop by Jeff Anderson. Copyright © 2005. Stenhouse Publishers. All rights reserved.

Mechanically Inclined: Building Grammar, Usage, and Style into Writer's Workshop by Jeff Anderson. Copyright © 2005. Stenhouse Publishers. All rights reserved.

Three Basic Complex Sentence Pattern Visual Scaffolds

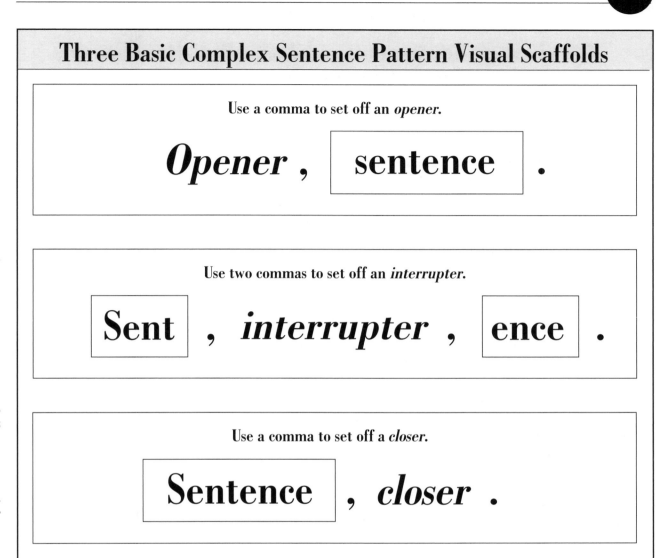

Use a comma to set off an *opener.*

Opener , | sentence | .

Use two commas to set off an *interrupter.*

| Sent | , *interrupter* , | ence | .

Use a comma to set off a *closer.*

| Sentence | , *closer* .

Inspired by Carroll and Wilson's *Acts of Teaching* (1993).

Comma Reinforcers: Cut-and-Paste Mini-Handbooks for the Writer's Notebook

Participles

Participles are *-ing* verbs and *-ed* verbs that evoke action and movement in our sentences, either to start a phrase or have a series. (Participles can be *-en* verbs, too.)

Wishing it were cooler and **wishing** she weren't **hungry,** *Franny Davis stood in line at the school cafeteria door,* **fingering** *the lunch pass in her pocket.* (p. 1)
—Mary Stolz, *The Noonday Friends*

The bus motor idles, **putting** **out a long tornado of blue smoke.** (p. 6)
—Chuck Palahniuk, *Choke*

Burping, growing, throwing, running—*everything is a race.* (p. 6)
—Jerry Spinelli, *Loser*

Absolute

- Noun + an *-ing, -ed,* or *-en,* verb (*lip quivering*)
- Noun + an adverb (*head down, hat off*)
- Noun + an adjective (*head sweaty, his shirt white and crisp*)
- Noun + a preposition (*pen in hand*)
- Preposition (usually *with* or *like*) + noun + any of the above variations (*With hair standing up on the back of her neck*)
- Possessive pronoun + noun + variations from above (*her breath soft*)

One morning I awoke before her and found her still asleep, **arms wrapped around his pillow, her breath soft, cat at her feet.** (p. 5)
—Kathy Appelt, *My Father's Summers*

"And on my honor," *Bear said,* **his voice booming, his arms spread wide.** (p. 172)
—Avi, *Crispin*

I sit by the door, **my knees drawn to my chest.** (p. 5)
Now he was walking toward us, **hands on hips, his sneakers kicking up little puffs of dust.** (p. 39)
—Khaled Hosseini, *The Kite Runner*

Mr. DeCuervo got out first, **his hair making him look like a giant dandelion.** (p. 3)
—Amy Bloom, "Love Is Not a Pie" in *Come to Me*

Appositives

An appositive acts as a second image for the noun that it renames. When you want to combine two sentences, appositives help you do it. Remember the basket test for the interrupter pattern.

Monsieur Bibot, **the dentist,** *was a very fussy man.* (p. 2)
—Chris Van Allsburg, *The Sweetest Fig*

Louis, **the yard teacher,** *frowned.* (p. 1)
—Louis Sachar, *Wayside School Is Falling Down*

Appositives can rename more than once:
What I wasn't used to was having his smell back, **the smoke from his Camel cigarettes, his Old Spice after-shave, the shoe polish he used on his boots.** (p. 29— They rename her dad's smells and are absolutes.)
—Kathi Appelt, *My Father's Summers*

Appositives can also be set off with dashes, especially when the appositive contains a comma.
Louie didn't seem to mind and belched softy— **a green drifter, the kind of belch that made people move away in a crowded room**—*and turned, waiting for next day delivery.* (p. 17)
—Gary Paulsen, *Harris and Me*

Mechanically Inclined: Building Grammar, Usage, and Style into Writer's Workshop by Jeff Anderson. Copyright © 2005. Stenhouse Publishers. All rights reserved.

Mechanically Inclined: Building Grammar, Usage, and Style into Writer's Workshop by Jeff Anderson. Copyright © 2005. Stenhouse Publishers. All rights reserved.

Adjectives Out of Order

Instead of using a long list of adjectives before a noun, shift a couple behind it.

We cruise past block after block of humble little houses, **whitewashed and stucco,** *built decades ago.* (p. 91)
—Eric Schlosser, *Fast Food Nation*

Nausea began to spread through his stomach, **warm and oozy and evil.** (p. 5)
He was aware of the other players around him, **helmeted and grotesque,** *creatures from an unknown world.* (p. 2)
—Robert Cormier, *The Chocolate War*

A drunk guy staggers into my field, **red-eyed and swearing.** (p. 2)
—Tracy Mack, *Birdland*

AAAWWUBBIS (As the First Word of a Sentence)

When an AAAWWUBBIS (*after, although, as, when, while, until, before, because, if,* or *since*) is the first word of a sentence, you're going to need a comma—usually. *Note:* We don't always use commas when an AAAWWUBBIS appears later in the sentence or if the phrase it's connected to is too short. Use your ear and good sense.

Before the plate hit the table, *Louie leaned forward like a snake striking and hit the stack of pancakes with his fork.* (p. 16)
—Gary Paulsen, *Harris and Me*

If there was an Olympic contest for talking, *Shelly Stalls would sweep the event.* (p. 16)
—Wendelin Van Draanen, *Flipped*

When I pop in a Bird CD, *it's like I feel myself filling up with Zeke.* (p. 66)
—Tracy Mack, *Birdland*

After working Winn-Dixie and I would go to the library to hear a story. (p. 98)
—Kate DiCamillo, *Because of Winn-Dixie*

Prepositional Phrases (When Used as Sentence Openers)

Between, in, over, to, under—prepositional phrases are sentence parts that start off with prepositions like these. See any list of common prepositions. Often when a prepositional phrase starts a sentence, it will act like an opener and take a comma before the main clause starts. Clarity is the game. If the comma is needed to set off the prepositional phrase, insert it. *Note:* We don't always use commas when a prepositional phrase appears late in the sentence. Use your ear and good sense. Consider deleting the comma if the prepositional phrase is not at the beginning of a sentence or is clearly part of the base clause.

With the possible exception of some species of sharks in a feeding frenzy, *I had never seen anything eat like Louie.* (p. 16)
—Gary Paulsen, *Harris and Me*

Outside my bedroom window, *a weeping willow tree tossed and switched its branches against the shingles on windy nights.* (p. 18)
—Wally Lamb, *She's Come Undone*

Her voice is rough, **like a bus grinding its breaks.** (p. 36)
He has sort of a sweet, tangy smell, **like a fresh orange slice dipped in vinegar.** (p. 74)
—Tracy Mack, *Birdland*

Christensen, Bonnie-Jean, and Francis Christensen. 1976. *A New Rhetoric.*
Christensen, Francis. 1967. *Notes Toward a New Rhetoric.*
Noden, Harry. 1999. *Image Grammar.* Portsmouth, NH: Heinemann.

More Than Anyone Wants to Know About Pronouns

Indefinite Pronouns (Have a Definite Number)

Singular	another, anybody, anyone, anything, each, either, everybody, everyone, everything, little, much, neither, nobody, no one, nothing, one, other, somebody, someone, something
Plural	both, few, many, others, several
Singular or Plural	all, any, more, most, none, some

Demonstrative Pronouns (Point to Nouns or Stand in for Them)

Singular	this, that
Plural	these, those

Reflexive Pronouns (Rename Subjects of Action Verbs)

Singular	myself, yourself, himself, herself, itself
Plural	ourselves, yourselves, themselves

Relative Pronouns (Relate Clauses to the Rest of the Sentence)

who, whoever, whose, whom, whomever
what ,whatever
which, whichever
that

Mechanically Inclined: Building Grammar, Usage, and Style into Writer's Workshop by Jeff Anderson. Copyright © 2005. Stenhouse Publishers. All rights reserved.

Mechanically Inclined: Building Grammar, Usage, and Style into Writer's Workshop by Jeff Anderson. Copyright © 2005. Stenhouse Publishers. All rights reserved.

Pronoun Agreement: A *Kira-Kira* Cloze

Put a pronoun in every blank. Make sure that the pronoun matches its antecedent (what the pronoun refers back to or stands in for).

_____ sister, Lynn, taught me _____ first word: kira-kira. I pronounced _____ ka-a-ahhh, but _____ knew what I meant. Kira-kira means "glittering" in Japanese. Lynn told _____ that when I was a baby, _____ used to take me onto our empty road at night, where we would lie on _____ backs and look at the stars while she said over and over, "Katie, say 'kira-kira, kira-kira.'" _____ loved that word! When I grew older, _____ used kira-kira to describe _____ I liked: the beautiful blue sky, puppies, kittens, butterflies, colored Kleenex.

My mother said _____ were misusing the word; you could not call a Kleenex kira-kira. _____ was dismayed over how un-Japanese we were and vowed to send _____ to Japan one day. I didn't care where she sent me, so long as Lynn came along.

—Cynthia Kadohata, *Kira-Kira*

everything	she	I	it
I	My	us	we
she	our	me	She
my			

Pronoun Case Chart

Pronoun Case

Point of View	Subjective	Possessive	Objective	Number
First Person	I	my mine	me	Singular
	we	our	us	Plural
Second Person	you	your	you	Singular/Plural
Third Person	he she it	his hers its	him her it	Singular
	we they	our their	us them	Plural
	who	whose	whom	Singular/Plural

Pronoun Reminders

1. Pronouns are stand-ins for nouns
2. Whenever you use a pronoun, make sure it has a clear antecedent (the noun it is substituting for)
3. Make sure pronouns match the number, person, and gender of their antecedents
   - number—singular or plural
   - person—point of view
   - gender—male or female
4. Point of view creates a tone
   - First person—involved
   - Second person—conversational
   - Third person—removed observer (in fiction omniscient, in nonfiction objective)
5. Some indefinite pronouns: *all, each, everyone, nobody, some* and *somebody*
6. Indefinite-demonstrative pronouns: *whomever, whatever, whoever*
7. Singular pronouns that point to particular things: *this, that*
8. Plural pronouns that point to particular things: *these, those*
9. Is anyone still reading?

Mechanically Inclined: Building Grammar, Usage, and Style into Writer's Workshop by Jeff Anderson. Copyright © 2005. Stenhouse Publishers. All rights reserved.

Mechanically Inclined: Building Grammar, Usage, and Style into Writer's Workshop by Jeff Anderson. Copyright © 2005. Stenhouse Publishers. All rights reserved.

Subject–Verb Agreement: In the Present and in the Past

"Right Now" or Present Tense Verbs

Point of View (Person)	Singular	Plural
I/we voice (1st)	I talk.	We talk.
You voice (2nd)	You talk.	You talk.
He/she/it voice (3rd)	**He talks; she talks.** **Add -s or -es to the verb.**	They talk.

Notice the pattern: Use the base verb every time, except when using the *he/she/it* voice, the third-person singular.

"Already Happened" or Past Tense Verbs

Point of View (Person)	Singular	Plural
I/we voice (1st)	I talked.	We talked.
You voice (2nd)	You talked.	You talked.
He/she/it voice (3rd)	He talked; she talked.	They talked.

Notice the pattern: We always add *-ed* to the base verb to show that the events already happened or are in the past.

Mechanically Inclined: Building Grammar, Usage, and Style into Writer's Workshop by Jeff Anderson. Copyright © 2005. Stenhouse Publishers. All rights reserved.

25 Irregular Verbs to Know

Present	Past	Past Participle
become	became	become
begin	began	begun
bring	brought	brought
buy	bought	bought
catch	caught	caught
come	came	come
cost	cost	cost
do	did	done
draw	drew	drawn
eat	ate	eaten
fall	fell	fallen
give	gave	given
go	went	gone
hear	heard	heard
keep	kept	kept
know	knew	known
make	made	made
run	ran	run
say	said	said
see	saw	seen
send	sent	sent
sing	sang	sung
take	took	taken
think	thought	thought
write	wrote	written

This short list of some of the most common irregular verbs was made using Diana Hacker's list of common irregular verbs and correlating them with the 500 most frequently used words found in Kylene Beers' *When Kids Can't Read* and a few that I often see misspelled in students' papers.

Mechanically Inclined: Building Grammar, Usage, and Style into Writer's Workshop by Jeff Anderson. Copyright © 2005. Stenhouse Publishers. All rights reserved.

Subject-Verb Agreement Examples

First- (*I/We*) and Second-Person (*You*) Singular and Plural

Singular first- and second-person subjects use the **base form** of the verb in the present tense. So does the *they* voice (third-person plural).

I *eat* as if I am starving, too.

We *eat* plenty.

You *eat* like a bird.

They *eat* pizza every Thursday.

Third-Person Singular (*He/She/It* Voice)

In the **present tense**, add *-s* or *-es* to the base verb when agreeing with singular third-person subjects.

Daniel, dog, book, he, she, it

My **dog** *eats* her kibble as if she were starving.

Anybody, anyone, each, every, everyone, much, no one, one, other, somebody, something

Anybody *can* write. In fact, **everyone** *is* writing.

Groups or collective nouns (team, family, class, crowd, etc.) and things acting as one thing or entity (mathematics, news)

The **crowd** *cheers* for the young writers.
The **news** of last night's game *spreads* through the campus.

Titles of written works or movies: *Charlotte's Web, The Incredibles*

The Tale of Despereaux tells the brave story of a tiny mouse with big ears.

Companies: Apple, Macy's

Apple *makes* the ipod.

Macy's *is* my favorite department store.

Use **does** and **has** with third-person singular as well: She *doesn't* care about this. She *has* it memorized.

Past Tense

Add *-ed* in all points of view (person). See exceptions in the charts for *do, have,* and *be* and the list of irregular verbs.

I *asked.*

You *asked.*

He *asked* an important question.

They *asked.*

Be Verbs: Present and Past

Be Verbs in the Present ("Right Now")

Point of View (Person)	Singular	Plural
I/we voice (1st)	I am intelligent.	We are intelligent.
You voice (2nd)	You are intelligent.	You are intelligent.
He/she/it voice (3rd)	He is intelligent; she is intelligent.	They are intelligent.

Be Verbs in the Past ("Already Happened")

Point of View (Person)	Singular	Plural
I/we voice (1st)	I was intelligent.	We were intelligent.
You voice (2nd)	You were intelligent.	You were intelligent.
He/she/it voice (3rd)	He was intelligent; she was intelligent.	They were intelligent.

Mechanically Inclined: Building Grammar, Usage, and Style into Writer's Workshop by Jeff Anderson. Copyright © 2005. Stenhouse Publishers. All rights reserved.

Mechanically Inclined: Building Grammar, Usage, and Style into Writer's Workshop by Jeff Anderson. Copyright © 2005. Stenhouse Publishers. All rights reserved.

Do and *Have* Verbs: Singular and Plural

Do Verbs

Present Tense ("Right Now")

Use *do* with every present tense form except the *he/she/it* voice, third-person singular. We do say *I do*, but we never say *she do*—we say *she does as he does* (think of *does* as the -s form of *do*).

Point of View (Person)	Singular	Plural
I/we voice (1st)	I do/don't	We do/don't
You voice (2nd)	You do/don't	You do/don't
He/she/it voice (3rd)	**He does/doesn't**	They do/don't
	She does/doesn't	Friends do/don't
	Elliot does/doesn't	

Notice the pattern: See how again it is the *he/she/it* voice that is the exception, just like most other verb patterns.

Past Tense ("Already happened")

Use **did/didn't** in all cases.

Have Verbs

Present Tense ("Right Now")

Have verbs follow the same patterns. Think of *has* as the -s form of *have*.

Point of View (Person)	Singular	Plural
I/we voice (1st)	I have/haven't	We have/haven't
You voice (2nd)	You have/haven't	You have/haven't
He/she/it voice (3rd)	**He has/hasn't**	They have/haven't
	She has/hasn't	Boys have/haven't
	Jericha has/hasn't	

Past Tense ("Already Happened")

Use **had/hadn't** in all cases.

Tense Cloze Activity

Walking into my Math class, I _____ the girl of my dreams sitting in the last desk of the first row. Her brown hair, swept to the right, _____ down on her shoulders. She _____ a bag of Doritos. Nacho cheese, my favorite. Could it get any better, I _____ to myself. And then she _____ at me. She _____ to speak to me. Her lips, outlined in brown, _____, "What are you looking at?" The sound of my dream deflating _____ in my ear.

see	saw
cascades	cascaded
eats	ate
thinks	thought
look	looked
is going	was going
open	opened
hisses	hissed

Mechanically Inclined: Building Grammar, Usage, and Style into Writer's Workshop by Jeff Anderson. Copyright © 2005. Stenhouse Publishers. All rights reserved.

Mechanically Inclined: Building Grammar, Usage, and Style into Writer's Workshop by Jeff Anderson. Copyright © 2005. Stenhouse Publishers. All rights reserved.

Transition Words (Conjunctive Adverbs)

Addition	*besides, finally, first, furthermore, in addition, last, moreover, next, still*
Comparison	*also, likewise, similarly*
Contrast	*even though, however, instead, nevertheless, on the other hand, otherwise, still, though, yet*
Example or Illustration	*after all, for example, for instance, in fact, in other words, in short, of course, specifically, to illustrate, thus*
Summary	*all in all, finally, in other words, therefore*
Time Sequence	*afterward, before, earlier, eventually, lately, meanwhile, next, now, since, soon, then, until*

Punctuation's Basic Functions

Separation	Mark	Job	Function
Maximum	Period	Ends a sentence	Separates independent clauses (sentences)
	Question mark	Indicates a question	
	Exclamation point	Shows excitement and extremes (pain, anger, joy)	
Medium	Semicolon	Acts like a softer period between sentences with linked ideas. Semicolons separate items in lists with items that contain commas.	Separates independent clauses (sentences) and elements in lists with internal punctuation
	Colon	Indicates anticipation (a drum roll)	Separates independent clauses or other elements from the independent clause
	Dash	Emphasis (think neon)	
Minimum	Comma	Commas separate items in a series or separate clauses or phrases from the core sentence.	Separates elements from independent clauses

Mechanically Inclined: Building Grammar, Usage, and Style into Writer's Workshop by Jeff Anderson. Copyright © 2005. Stenhouse Publishers. All rights reserved.

Mechanically Inclined: Building Grammar, Usage, and Style into Writer's Workshop by Jeff Anderson. Copyright © 2005. Stenhouse Publishers. All rights reserved.

Alphabetical Punctuation Guide

Punctuation	Name	Meaning/Purpose	Background and Tips
&	Ampersand	Shorthand *and*	I learned the word watching *Wheel of Fortune*. The ampersand was invented as a spacesaver in the 1700s and was used frequently for a time. Now its use is confined to names that contain it like A&W Root Beer and puzzles on *Wheel of Fortune*. *My cell phone was with AT&T.*
'	Apostrophe	Shows possession or contraction or deleted letters	Like a raised comma, the apostrophe means so much: • shows possession (*Concheeta's pencil, book's cover*) • shows a contraction or deletion of letters (*Don't do that 'cause it sounds funny.*)
:	Colon	Announces a surprise or a list; acts as a drum roll for something to follow	Capitalize the first word after a colon only if it's a proper noun or the start of a complete sentence.
,	Comma	Separates or joins	The comma, the most used punctuation mark, can: • separate items in a series • enclose asides or interrupters • join sentences when used with one of the FANBOYS • separate openers and closers from independent clauses or base sentences.
—	Dash	Shows a break in thought or sets off something with emphasis	The dash can often be replaced by a comma, colon, semicolon, or parenthesis. Don't overuse our friend—the dash—as it will lose its emphatic effect.
. . .	Ellipsis	Indicates omission or hesitation	Always use three dots to show an ellipsis, unless you're ending a sentence with an ellipsis. Then add the period and it looks like four, but it's really three with a period. *Being on the LAM was a whole lot of fun . . . for about five minutes.* (p. 36) —Christopher Paul Curtis, *Bud, Not Buddy*
!	Exclamation point	Indicates extreme pain, fear, astonishment, anger, disgust, or yelling	Don't overuse exclamation points! Really!! Cut it out!!!

(continued)

—	Hyphen	Indicates that two words should be thought of as one, especially when using two adjectives or groups of words that are acting as a unit	Use hyphens to • join compound adjectives before a noun (*hard-working student*) • join compound nouns and two-word and multiple-word concepts (*mother-in-law, know-how, skin-deep*) • most sources no longer recommend hyphenating paired nationalities (*African American, Italian American*) • add a prefix to a word when clarity is needed or to avoid doubling vowels (anti-intellectual) • divide lettered words (*T-shirt, L-shaped, X-ray, U-turn*) • divide a word between syllables at the end of a line: *When in doubt about hyphen-ation, check your dictionary.*
( )	Parentheses	Indicate an aside or something nonessential (parenthetical)	Parentheses may be used for • clarification of technical or obscure terms • conversions or translations
•	Period	Indicates what the British call a "full stop." The sentence is over. Abbreviations and initials	*When you reach the period, it's all over.* (p. 134) —Patricia O'Conner, *Woe Is I* *Mr. Chips, Ms. Pacman, Dr. Pepper, or gov.* No periods between well-known initials like JFK or the CIA.
?	Question mark	Indicates, you guessed it, a question. It can also show doubt.	Need I say more? Genuine questions deserve their mark. Don't use a question mark for indirect questions: *The principal is always asking me questions.*
" "	Quotation marks	Encloses direct speech or direct quotes from sources	*"Dialogue brings writing to life,"* said the student. To indicate a quote within a quote, use single quotation marks to enclose it.
;	Semicolon	Links independent clauses with similar ideas. May be needed when there are already too many commas in a sentence	Between the period and the comma lies the semicolon. When items in a series contain commas, use a semicolon for clarity.
/	Slash	Shows the end of a line in quoted poetry and may be used to separate alternatives like *either/or.*	Though the slash is used in legal documents, most mavens refrain from using it in prose, unless showing line endings in poetry. For example, dealing with the gender issue by inserting *his/her* will get a rise out of many a maven.
:-)	Smiley face and other emoticons	Indicate emotions	Don't use an emoticon in writing other than an e-mail, a sticky note, or an extremely informal communication :-)

Cappon, Rene J. 2003. *The Associated Press Guide to Punctuation*. New York: Basic Books.
Cleveland, Ceil. 2002. *Better Punctuation in 30 Minutes a Day*. New York: Barnes and Noble Books.

Mechanically Inclined: Building Grammar, Usage, and Style into Writer's Workshop by Jeff Anderson. Copyright © 2005. Stenhouse Publishers. All rights reserved.

Glossary

AAAWWUBBIS A mnemonic that helps students (and me) remember the most common subordinating conjunctions.

Absolute The absolute construction is not a sentence on its own, but contains a noun and either a verb, preposition, or adjective.

Adjective Word that describes or modifies nouns and pronouns.

Adjectives out of order Shifting adjectives behind the noun they describe.

Appositive A word or group of words that rename a noun in the sentence, acting like a second noun. Usually appositives are considered nonessential information, so they are set off with commas. *Dash, a fast runner, helped save his family.*

Clause Contains a subject and a verb. See *dependent clause* and *independent clause.*

Closer A group of words that are not a sentence on their own placed at the end of an independent clause after a comma.

Conventions Agreements, customs, and rules followed by a society or group of people. In language, conventions are agreements between writers and readers—punctuation, capitalization, paragraphing, grammar, and mechanics.

Comma splice	Two independent clauses joined with only a comma and no coordinating conjunction: *The fountain sounded great, it needs to be cleaned.* Comma splices can be fixed three ways: Change the comma to a period, add a coordinating conjunction after the comma, or change the comma to a semicolon.
Complex sentence	One or more dependent clauses joined with an independent clause. *Whenever I write, I find out all sorts of things.*
Compound sentence	Two or more sentences joined with a comma and a coordinating conjunction or a semicolon. *Write with your senses, **and** write with your heart. Write with your senses; write with your heart.*
Conjunctions	Words that connect sentence parts. See *coordinating conjunctions* and *subordinating conjunctions.*
Connecter	Words or phrases that connect other words or ideas. Subordinating and coordinating conjunctions are connectors.
Coordinating conjunctions	Coordinating conjunctions such as *for, and, nor, but, or, yet, so* (FANBOYS) link ideas that are usually equal. A coordinating conjunction may join two independent clauses: *She is right, and I am wrong.* But, sometimes coordinating conjunctions are used to join words or phrases: *I like apples and bananas. She really should stop marking up all the errors and seeing only what is wrong with their writing.*
Dangling modifier	Placing a modifier in the wrong place, or not modifying the subject of the sentence, which confuses the meaning of the message, is a dangling modifier. Incorrect examples: *Deprived of coffee, the papers remained ungraded.* Correct example: *Deprived of coffee, the English teacher was unable to grade the papers.*
Dependent clause	A clause that contains a noun and a verb but does not express a complete thought. Example: *Since I was in fourth grade.*
Essential clauses	See *restrictive clauses.*
FANBOYS	A mnemonic to remember the coordinating conjunctions *for, and, nor, but, or, yet, so.*
Fragment	An incomplete sentence that is punctuated like a sentence but is missing either a subject or a verb and does not communicate a complete thought.
Free modifier	In theory, the placement of this modifier doesn't matter. In reality, we should always make sure that our sentences make sense and our modifiers don't dangle.
Independent clause	A clause containing both a subject and a verb and expressing a complete thought.
Inflectional endings	The suffixes *-s, -es, -ing, -ed* added to the ends of verbs to reveal when an event occurs or occurred. Students often drop inflectional endings, which causes agreement and tense problems.
Interrupter	Any word or group of words that interrupt a sentence and require a comma on both sides.

Modifier	A word, phrase, or clause that modifies or changes a noun, verb, or entire sentence by adding information. Adjectives and adverbs are modifiers.
Nonessential clauses	See *nonrestrictive clauses.*
Nonrestrictive or nonessential clauses	Clauses that add information that is not essential to the meaning. These clauses are set off with a comma or commas if they interrupt a sentence.
Noun	Person, place, thing, or idea.
Opener	Any introductory element that is set off with a comma. An opener could be an adverb, phrase, or dependent clause—any unit that could not stand on its own as a sentence. An opener is attached at the beginning of the sentence. *In the background, I hear Linda Ronstadt records. Softly, her hand touches mine.*
Parallelism	Using the same word, structure, or rhythm to create a sense of music, emphasis, and fluency.
Participles	Defined by Harry Noden as an *-ing* verb, a participle is a form of a verb. A participle can also be an *-ed* verb or any verb in past tense (past participle). *Deprived of coffee, the English teacher was unable to grade her 150 essays.* The present participle is the *-ing* form. *Dripping with sweat, Alex used half a box of tissues to dry himself.*
Phrase	A group of words that form a unit of meaning. A phrase does not contain its own subject and verb.
Point of view	The perspective of the writer: first person (*I, we*); second person (*you*); or third person (*he/she/it* or *they*).
Preposition	Words like *over, under, of,* and *with,* which show relationships between words in a sentence. For a list of common prepositions, see page 163.
Prepositional phrase	A group of words that begins with a preposition and ends with a noun or pronoun. A prepositional phrase does not contain a verb.
Pronoun case	The form pronouns take in a sentence, based on their function. In the subjective case, a pronoun acts as the subject of the sentence: *I like reading books about true things.* In the possessive case, the pronoun shows ownership: *I can't wait to finish my book.* In the objective case, the pronoun must receive some sort of action: *Please give that book to me.* See lesson on pronoun case, page 172.
Punctuation	Anything that helps group sentences or words together or split them apart.
Restrictive or essential clauses	Clauses that must be in the sentence for it to be a complete sentence. Without the restrictive clause, the sentence's meaning would be altered completely. *The man who stole our wind chimes just walked past the house.* If we took out the phrase *who stole our wind chimes,* the sentence would read *The man just walked past the house.* The foreboding meaning would be lost; thus, we do not insert commas around this phrase because it is essential to the sentence's meaning.

Run-on sentence　Two or more sentences joined as one unit without any proper punctuation—sometimes referred to as a comma splice.

Sentence part　Any unit of a sentence that does not make a sentence on its own.

Subject　Who or what the sentence is about.

Subject-verb agreement　Subjects agree with their verbs in number, person, and case.

Subordinate clause　See *dependent clause* and *subordinating conjunctions* (AAAWWUBBIS).

Subordinating conjunctions　Subordinating conjunctions such as *after, although, as, when, while, until, because, before, if,* and *since* (AAAWWUBBIS) create dependent clauses when they are used as head words. *Since I used a coordinating conjunction at the beginning of this sentence, I must use a comma to set off the introductory element.*

Subordination　Connecting two unequal but related ideas using a subordinating conjunction. See *AAAWWUBBIS.*

Syntax　The arrangement of words in sentences—the flow, the pattern, the grammatical structures. Originates from the Greek *syn,* meaning together, and *taxis,* meaning sequence or order.

Verb　An action word that changes depending on the time in which it occurs—present, past, or future. *I **run** to the bathroom. I **ran** to the bathroom. I **will run** to the bathroom again—and again.*

References

Amis, Kingsley. 1997. *The King's English: A Guide to Modern Usage*. New York: St. Martin's Press.

Anderson, Carl. 2000. *How's It Going? A Practical Guide to Conferring with Student Writers*. Portsmouth, NH: Heinemann.

Anderson, Jeff. 2003. "Naming Names: A Concrete Way to Help Students Write." *Voices from the Middle* 11 (2): 27–31.

Anderson, Laurie Halse. 2001. *Speak*. New York: Puffin.

Angelillo, Janet. 2002. *A Fresh Approach to Teaching Punctuation*. New York: Scholastic.

Appelt, Kathi. 2004. *My Father's Summers: A Daughter's Memoir*. New York: Henry Holt.

Atwell, Nancie. 1998. *In the Middle: New Understandings About Reading, Writing, and Learning*. Portsmouth, NH: Heinemann.

———. 2002. *Lessons That Change Writers*. Portsmouth, NH: Heinemann.

Avi. 2002. *Crispin: The Cross of Lead*. New York: Hyperion.

Babbit, Natalie. 1985. *Tuck Everlasting*. New York: Farrar, Straus, and Giroux.

Barclay, Jane. 2003. *How Hot Was It?* Montreal: Lobster Press.

Baylor, Byrd. 1997. *The Other Way to Listen*. New York: Aladdin Books.

Beers, Kylene. 2002. *When Kids Can't Read: What Teachers Can Do*. Portsmouth, NH: Heinemann.

Bernabei, Gretchen. 2005. *Reviving the Essay: How to Teach Structure Without Formula*. Shoreham, VT: Discover Writing.

Berne, Suzanne. 1998. *A Crime in the Neighborhood*. New York: Henry Holt.

Bernstein, Theodore. 1998. *The Careful Writer: A Modern Guide to English Usage*. New York: Free Press.

Bitton-Jackson, Livia. 1999. *I Have Lived a Thousand Years: Growing Up in the Holocaust*. New York: Simon Pulse.

Block, Francesca Lia. 2001. *The Rose and the Beast: Fairy Tales Retold*. New York: Joanna Cotler Books.

Bloom, Amy. 1994. "Love Is Not a Pie." In *Come to Me: Stories*. New York: Perennial Books.

Caine, Renate Nummela, and Geoffrey Caine. 1994. *Making Connections: Teaching and the Human Brain*. New York: Dale Seymour Publications.

Calkins, Lucy. 2003. *Units of Study for Primary Writing.* Portsmouth, NH: Heinemann.

Cambourne, Brian. 1988. *The Whole Story: Natural Learning and the Acquisition of Literacy.* New York: Scholastic.

Cambourne, Brian, and Hazel Brown. 1990. *Read and Retell.* Portsmouth, NH: Heinemann.

Capote, Truman. 1994. *Other Voices, Other Rooms.* New York: Vintage.

Cappon, Rene J. 2003. *The Associated Press Guide to Punctuation.* New York: Perseus.

Carroll, Joyce Armstrong, and Edward E. Wilson. 1993. *Acts of Teaching: How to Teach Writing.* Englewood Cliffs, NJ: Teacher Idea Press.

Choldenko, Gennifer. 2004. *Al Capone Does My Shirts.* New York: Putnam Juvenile.

Christensen, Francis. 1968. *Notes Toward a New Rhetoric: Six Essays for Teachers.* New York: Harper and Row.

Christensen, Francis, and Bonnijean Christensen. 1976. *A New Rhetoric.* New York: Harper and Row.

Cisneros, Sandra. 1984. *The House on Mango Street.* New York: Knopf.

———. 1997. *Hairs/Pelitos.* New York: Dragonfly Books.

Clements, Andrew. 1998. *Frindle.* New York: Aladdin Books.

Cleveland, Ceil. 2002. *Better Punctuation in 30 Minutes a Day.* Franklin Lakes, NJ: Career Press.

Connors, Robert J., and Andrea Lunsford. 1988. "Frequency of Formal Errors in Current College Writing, or Ma and Pa Kettle Do Research." *College Composition and Communication* 39: 395–409.

———. 1997. *The Everyday Writer: A Brief Reference.* New York: St. Martin's Press.

Cormier, Robert. 1974. *The Chocolate War.* New York: Random House.

Cowell, Cressida. 2005. *How to Be a Pirate.* New York: Little, Brown.

Curtis, Christopher Paul. 2000. *Bud, Not Buddy.* New York: Yearling Books.

Curtis, Jamie Lee. 1993. *When I Was Little: A Four-Year-Old's Memoir of Her Youth.* New York: Joanna Cotler Books.

Dahl, Roald. 1998. *Matilda.* New York: Puffin Books.

———. 2001. *Boy: Tales of Childhood.* New York: Puffin Books.

Danzinger, Paula. 1998. *The Cat Ate My Gymsuit.* New York: Putnam Juvenile.

Dawkins, John. 1995. "Teaching Punctuation as a Rhetorical Tool." *College Composition and Communication* 46: 533–48.

DiCamillo, Kate. 2001. *Because of Winn-Dixie.* Cambridge, MA: Candlewick.

———. 2003. *The Tale of Despereaux.* Cambridge, MA: Candlewick.

Dixon, Franklin W. 1990. *The Dead Season.* New York: Simon Pulse.

Donnelly, Jennifer. 2004. *A Northern Light.* New York: Harcourt.

Elbow, Peter. 1998a. *Writing Without Teachers.* New York: Oxford University Press.

———. 1998b. *Writing with Power.* New York: Oxford University Press.

Farmer, Nancy. 2004. *The House of the Scorpion.* New York: Simon & Schuster.

Fleischman, Paul. 1999. *Whirligig.* New York: Random House.

Fletcher, Ralph. 1996a. *A Writer's Notebook: Unlocking the Writer Within You.* New York: Avon Books.

———. 1996b. *Breathing In, Breathing Out: Keeping a Writer's Notebook.* Portsmouth, NH: Heinemann.

Foxworthy, Jeff. 2004. *You Might Be a Redneck If . . . This Is the Biggest Book You've Ever Read.* Nashville, TN: Rutledge Hill Press.

Franzen, Jonathan. 2001. *The Corrections: A Novel.* New York: Farrar, Straus and Giroux.

Freedman, Russell. 2004. *The Voice That Challenged a Nation: Marion Anderson and the Struggle for Equal Rights*. Boston: Houghton Mifflin.

———. 1989. *Lincoln: A Photobiography*. Boston: Houghton Mifflin.

Friedman, Kinky. 2003. *Kinky Friedman's Guide to Texas Etiquette*. New York: Perennial Currents.

Gantos, Jack. 1995. *Heads or Tails: Stories from the Sixth Grade*. New York: Farrar, Straus and Giroux.

Giff, Patricia Reilly. 2002. *Pictures of Hollis Woods*. New York: Wendy Lamb Books.

Goldberg, Myla. 2001. *The Bee Season*. New York: Anchor Books.

Goldberg, Natalie. 1990. *Wild Mind: Living the Writer's Life*. New York: Bantam Books.

Gordon, Karen Elizabeth. 1993a. *The Deluxe Intransitive Vampire: The Ultimate Handbook of Grammar for the Innocent, the Eager, and the Doomed*. New York: Pantheon Books.

———. 1993b. *The New Well-Tempered Sentence: A Punctuation Handbook for the Innocent, the Eager, and the Doomed*. Boston: Houghton Mifflin.

Grealy, Lucy. 1994. *Autobiography of a Face*. Boston: Houghton Mifflin.

Grimsley, Jim. 1996. *Winter Birds*. New York: Simon & Schuster.

Hacker, Diane. 2003. *A Writer's Reference, Fifth Edition*. Boston: Bedford Books.

Hale, Constance. 1999. *Sin and Syntax: How to Craft Wickedly Effective Prose*. New York: Random House.

Hale, Marian. 2004. *The Truth About Sparrows*. New York: Henry Holt.

Harste, Jerome, Virginia Woodward, and Carolyn Burke. 1984. *Language Stories and Literacy Lessons*. Portsmouth, NH: Heinemann.

Hart, Leslie. 2002. *Human Brain and Human Learning*. Covington, WA: Books for Educators.

Harwayne, Shelley. 1992. *Lasting Impressions: Weaving Literature into the Writing Workshop*. Portsmouth, NH: Heinemann.

Hiassen, Carl. 2004. *Hoot*. New York: Knopf.

Hosseini, Khaled. 2003. *The Kite Runner*. New York: Riverhead Books.

Howe, James. 2001. *Howliday Inn*. New York: Aladdin Books.

———. 2002. *The Celery Stalks at Midnight*. New York: Simon & Schuster.

———. 2003. *The Misfits*. New York: Aladdin Books.

Hurston, Zora Neale. 1998. *Their Eyes Were Watching God*. New York: HarperCollins.

Junker, Howard, ed. 1995. *The Writer's Notebook*. New York: HarperCollins.

Kadohata, Cynthia. 2004. *Kira-Kira*. New York: Simon & Schuster.

Killgallon, Don. 1998. *Sentence Composing for High School*. Portsmouth, NH: Boynton/Cook.

Killgallon, Don, and Jenny Killgallon. 2000. *Sentence Composing for Elementary School*. Portsmouth, NH: Heinemann.

King, Stephen. 1982. *Cujo*. New York: Signet.

Klass, David. 2001. *You Don't Know Me*. New York: Farrar, Straus and Giroux.

Konigsburg, E. L. 2004. *The Outcasts of 19 Schuyler Place*. New York: Simon & Schuster.

Korman, Gordon. 2000. *No More Dead Dogs*. New York: Hyperion.

Lamb, Wally. 1998. *She's Come Undone*. New York: Simon & Schuster.

Lane, Barry. 1992. *After THE END: Teaching and Learning Creative Revision*. Portsmouth, NH: Heinemann.

Larson, Erik. 2003. *The Devil in the White City*. New York: Random House.

Lederer, Richard. 1989. *Anguished English: An Anthology of Accidental Assaults Upon Our Language*. New York: Random House.

Mack, Tracy. 2003. *Birdland*. New York: Scholastic.

MacLachlan, Patricia. 1993. *Journey*. New York: Bantam Doubleday Dell.

McCormick, Patricia. 2002. *Cut*. New York: Scholastic.

McDonald, Megan. 2000. *Judy Moody*. Cambridge, MA: Candlewick.

———. 2003. *Judy Moody Gets Famous!* Cambridge, MA: Candlewick.

Moffett, James. 1987. *Teaching the Universe of Discourse*. Portsmouth, NH: Boynton/Cook.

Morris, Alana. 1998. "Neurocentric Grammar." Presented at the New Jersey Writing Project in Texas.

Murphy, Jim. 2003. *An American Plague: The True and Terrifying Story of the Yellow Fever Epidemic of 1793*. New York: Clarion.

Murray, Donald. 1995. *The Craft of Revision*. New York: Harcourt.

Naylor, Phyllis Reynolds. 2000. *Shiloh*. New York: Aladdin Books.

Nixon, Joan Lowery. 1994. *Shadowmaker*. New York: Delacorte Books for Young Readers.

Noden, Harry. 1999. *Image Grammar: Using Grammatical Structures to Teach Writing*. Portsmouth, NH: Boynton/Cook.

Nye, Naomi Shihab. 1999. *Habibi*. New York: Simon & Schuster.

O'Conner, Patricia. 1996. *Woe Is I: The Grammarphobe's Guide to Better English in Plain English*. New York: Putnam.

———. 1999. *Words Fail Me: What Everyone Who Writes Should Know About Writing*. New York: Harcourt.

Orlean, Susan. 2000. *The Orchid Thief: A True Story of Beauty and Obsession*. New York: Ballantine Books.

Osa, Nancy. 2005. *Cuba 15*. New York: Random House.

Palahniuk, Chuck. 2002. *Choke*. New York: Anchor Books.

———. 2003. *Diary: A Novel*. New York: Doubleday.

Palatini, Margie. 2000. *Bedhead*. New York: Simon & Schuster.

Parkes, M. B. 1993. *Pause and Effect*. Berkeley: University of California Press.

Paterson, Katherine. 2004. *Bridge to Terabithia*. New York: HarperCollins.

Paulsen, Gary. 1995. *Harris and Me: A Summer Remembered*. New York: Bantam Doubleday Dell.

Peck, Richard. 2004. *The Teacher's Funeral: A Comedy in Three Parts*. New York: Dial Books.

Pelham, David, and Michael Foreman. 1989. *Worms Wiggle*. New York: Simon & Schuster.

Provost, Gary. 1990. *Make Your Words Work*. New York: Writer's Digest.

Pulver, Robin. 2003. *Punctuation Takes a Vacation*. New York: Holiday House.

Rawls, Wilson. 1998. *Summer of the Monkeys*. New York: Bantam Doubleday Dell.

Ray, Katie Wood. 2002. *What You Know by Heart: How to Develop Curriculum for Your Writing Workshop*. Portsmouth, NH: Heinemann.

Rice, David. 1996. *Give the Pig a Chance and Other Stories*. Tempe, AZ: Bilingual Press.

Rozakis, Laurie E. 2003. *The Complete Idiot's Guide to Grammar and Style*. New York: Alpha Books.

Rylant, Cynthia. 1996. *A Fine White Dust*. New York: Aladdin Books.

Sachar, Louis. 1987. *There's a Boy in the Girl's Bathroom*. New York: Random House.

———. 1998. *Wayside School Is Falling Down*. New York: Avon.

Schlosser, Eric. 2002. *Fast Food Nation: The Dark Side of the All-American Meal*. New York: Perennial.

Schmidt, Gary D. 2004. *Lizzie Bright and the Buckminster Boy*. New York: Clarion.

Schwartz, Alvin. 1981. *Scary Stories to Tell in the Dark*. New York: HarperCollins.

Shan, Darren. 2004. *Cirque Du Freak #6: The Vampire Prince*. New York: Little, Brown.

Shaughnessy, Mina. 1977. *Errors and Expectations: A Guide for the Teacher of Basic Writing*. New York: Oxford University Press.

Shreve, Susan. 2003. *Blister*. New York: Scholastic.

Spandel, Vicki. 2003. *Creating Young Writers*. Boston: Allyn and Bacon.

———. 2005. *Creating Writers Through 6-Trait Assessment and Instruction*. Boston: Allyn and Bacon.

Spinelli, Jerry. 2002. *Stargirl*. New York: Knopf.

———. 2003. *Loser*. New York: HarperCollins.

Stolz, Mary. 1993. *The Noonday Friends*. New York: HarperCollins.

Strong, William. 1994. *Sentence Combining: A Composing Book*. New York: McGraw-Hill.

———. 2001. *Coaching Writing: The Power of Guided Practice*. Portsmouth, NH: Heinemann.

Strunk, William, and E. B. White. 2000. *The Elements of Style*. Boston: Allyn and Bacon.

Tashjian, Janet. 2001. *The Gospel According to Larry*. New York: Henry Holt.

Thomas, Pat. 2000. "Mining for Gems: The Making of Readers and Writers." *Voices from the Middle* 8 (2): 26–33.

Thomas, Rob. 1998. *Slave Day*. New York: Simon & Schuster.

Tolan, Stephanie S. 2002. *Surviving the Applewhites*. New York: HarperCollins.

Trimble, John R. 1999. *Writing with Style: Conversations on the Art of Writing*. Columbus, OH: Prentice Hall.

Truss, Lynne. 2004. *Eats, Shoots & Leaves: The Zero Tolerance Approach to Punctuation*. New York: Gotham.

Van Allsburg, Chris. 1993. *The Sweetest Fig*. Boston: Houghton Mifflin.

Van Draanen, Wendelin. 2001. *Flipped*. New York: Knopf.

Vega, Denise. 2005. *Click Here: To Find Out How I Survived Seventh Grade*. New York: Little, Brown.

Venolia, Jan. 2001. *Write Right: A Desktop Digest of Punctuation, Grammar, and Style*. Berkeley, CA: Ten Speed Press.

Vygotsky, Lev. 1986. *Thought and Language*. Cambridge, MA: MIT Press.

Walsh, Bill. 2000. *Lapsing Into a Comma: A Curmudgeon's Guide to the Many Things That Can Go Wrong in Print—and How to Avoid Them*. Chicago: Contemporary Books.

———. 2004. *The Elephants of Style: A Trunkload of Tips on the Big Issues and Gray Areas of Contemporary American English*. Chicago: McGraw-Hill.

Weaver, Constance. 1996. *Teaching Grammar in Context*. Portsmouth, NH: Boynton/Cook.

———. 1998. *Lessons to Share on Teaching Grammar in Context*. Portsmouth, NH: Boynton/Cook.

White, E. B. 1974. *Charlotte's Web*. New York: HarperTrophy.

Willems, Mo. 2004. *Knuffle Bunny: A Cautionary Tale*. New York: Hyperion.

Woods, Geraldine. 2001. *English Grammar for Dummies*. New York: Hungry Minds.

Yep, Laurence. 1992. *The Star Fisher*. New York: Penguin.

Yolen, Jane. 1997. *Sleeping Ugly*. New York: Putnam.

Zinsser, William. 2001. *On Writing Well, 25th Anniversary Edition*. New York: HarperCollins.

Index